I N THE SPRING OF 1957, my father was offered a job in America. Since we lived in England, driving to work would have been something of a challenge unless we first crossed the Atlantic Ocean.

You could have asked me anything about castles, knights in armor, *The Wind in the Willows*, and the steam ships *Queen Elizabeth* (two funnels) and *Queen Mary* (three).

But all I knew about America was cowboys on horseback, which I saw on our small black-and-white television, and the Empire State Building. A colorful illustration in my *Encyclopedia of Science for Boys and Girls* made it look bigger than all the other buildings put together—much bigger.

I couldn't wait to see it with my own eyes.

I suppose my parents were busy applying for passports and visas and making lists. But with the exception of having our chests x-rayed to make sure we were healthy, life for my sister and brother and me went on as if nothing exciting was about to happen. Things only became a little more real when it was time to decide what we would take with us and what we had to leave behind. Everything we chose, including my mother's brand-new carpet, had to fit into a pair of steamer trunks we'd bought from a family of recent arrivals to England. They were large and covered with stickers (the trunks, not the family).

We children were limited to just three books each. My *Encyclopedia of Science* and an illustrated *Robinson Crusoe* that showed how to make furniture from a shipwreck were easy choices—and very practical. But then I had to decide between a thick book of airplane silhouettes and a thin book called *Ned, the Lonely Donkey*. After my desperate plea to take both was denied, Ned got the nod.

Four months after news of our upcoming adventure had broken and the last pieces of furniture had either been sold or given away, we left our house, friends, and neighbors and moved in with my grandparents. At last, inch by inch, I could feel the Empire State Building getting closer. Four weeks later, my father flew off to begin his new job and set up our apartment. A month after that, it was time to board the ship for the five-day voyage that would reunite the Macaulay family in the New World.

The whole process had taken forever. But as it turns out, preparations for our journey had been under way for much longer than I had realized.

DAVID MACAULAY

CROSSING on TIME

STEAM ENGINES, FAST SHIPS, AND A JOURNEY TO THE NEW WORLD

 Roaring Brook Press / New York

1

BEFORE THE 1800s, ships crossing the Atlantic Ocean were powered by the wind in their sails. But since the wind didn't always cooperate, it was difficult for shipowners to attract passengers. They couldn't predict how long a voyage might take or even when it would begin, and once under way there was no guarantee that the wind would keep blowing or that it wouldn't blow too much and turn the trip into a disaster. Until a more reliable source of power could be found, these crossings would remain a challenge to anyone, but particularly to the faint of heart and those on a tight schedule.

Shipping wasn't the only business needing a new source of power. For centuries, flooding in underground shafts and tunnels had made mining even more unpleasant and dangerous than it already was. Pumps along with a variety of inefficient contraptions were used to remove the unwanted water, but they depended on humans, animals, water, or wind to operate. Mine owners were desperate for a better solution.

A hand-operated pump can lift water only about 30 feet. To remove water from farther down would require several pumps on different levels operated either individually or all together by strong horses turning a wheel-like contraption (called a gin).

During the 1600s, scientists in England and Europe began experimenting with ways of putting vacuums and atmospheric pressure to work. They often used a cylinder sealed at the bottom and a piston that could slide up and down inside. When a vacuum was created beneath the piston, the pressure of the surrounding air would push it down into the cylinder. If a rope was connected between the piston and a weight, the movement of the piston could lift the weight off the ground. Different methods were used to create the vacuum, but each time the process had to begin from scratch. The problem was how to make the piston move up and down repeatedly inside the cylinder.

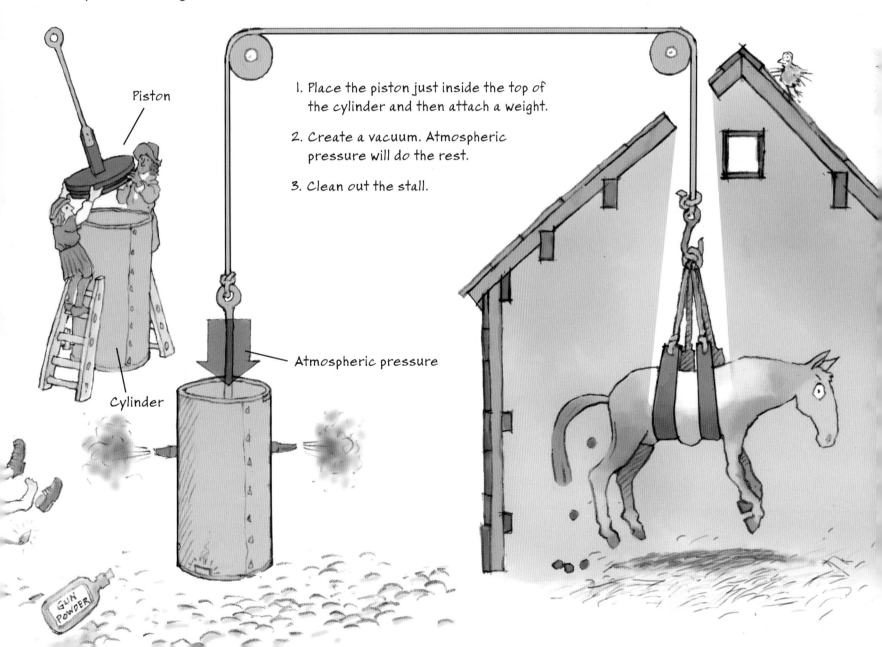

Piston

1. Place the piston just inside the top of the cylinder and then attach a weight.

2. Create a vacuum. Atmospheric pressure will do the rest.

3. Clean out the stall.

Atmospheric pressure

Cylinder

GUN POWDER

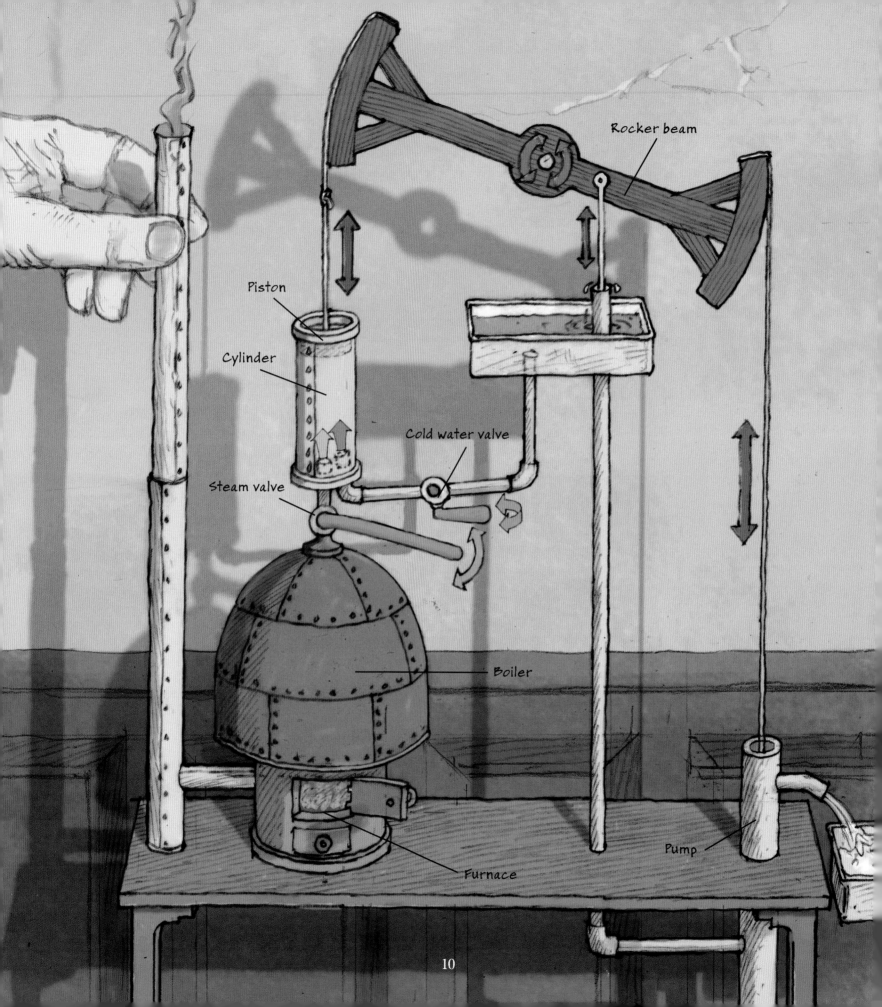

Rocker beam

Piston

Cylinder

Cold water valve

Steam valve

Boiler

Furnace

Pump

Around 1710 an English ironmonger, preacher, and inventor named Thomas Newcomen solved the miners' dilemma. By building on these early experiments, he was able to create the world's first continuously operating steam engine.

Newcomen's invention consumed an enormous amount of coal, but that didn't matter as long as it was put to work near a coal mine, and its ability to pump water from as far down as 150 feet made it a great success on both sides of the English Channel.

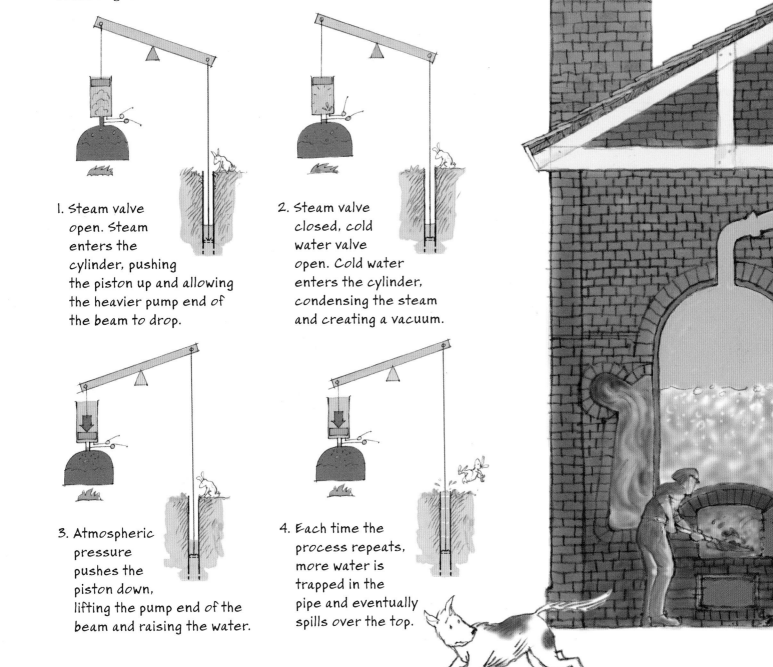

1. Steam valve open. Steam enters the cylinder, pushing the piston up and allowing the heavier pump end of the beam to drop.

2. Steam valve closed, cold water valve open. Cold water enters the cylinder, condensing the steam and creating a vacuum.

3. Atmospheric pressure pushes the piston down, lifting the pump end of the beam and raising the water.

4. Each time the process repeats, more water is trapped in the pipe and eventually spills over the top.

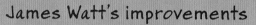

James Watt's improvements

1. To increase the power of the engine, Watt applied steam alternately to both sides of the piston.

2. To save fuel by not having to reheat the main cylinder between every stroke, he introduced a separate cylinder in which the exhausted steam was condensed.

3. To keep the main cylinder as hot as possible, he created a "blanket" around it filled with steam.

4. To reduce uneven wear, he designed an apparatus that ensured that the piston moved straight up and down in the cylinder.

1770 Nicholas-Joseph Cugnot, an engineer in the French army, built a three-wheeled steam-powered vehicle to carry cannons. The weight of the furnace and boiler at the front of the vehicle made it difficult to steer, particularly off-road, where battles tend to happen, so the army decided to stick with horses.

1783 Claude-François-Dorothée of France was the first person to successfully demonstrate a steam-powered paddleboat. Although he was unable to continue his work for lack of funding, the idea quickly spread.

As with almost every successful idea, Newcomen's engine was soon being improved upon by others. Many of the best ideas belonged to a Scottish inventor named James Watt. He and his business partner Matthew Boulton developed more powerful, efficient, and reliable steam engines that would drive machinery in Britain and Europe, and eventually on the other side of the Atlantic in the United States.

One of the most significant adaptations was the addition of a wheel to convert the up-and-down movement of the piston into rotary motion. From pumping water out of the mines, steam engines found their way into textile mills, foundries, and flour mills—and even into the world of transportation.

1784 William Murdoch's three-wheeled vehicle included a sliding valve that automatically directed steam first to one side of the piston and then to the other.

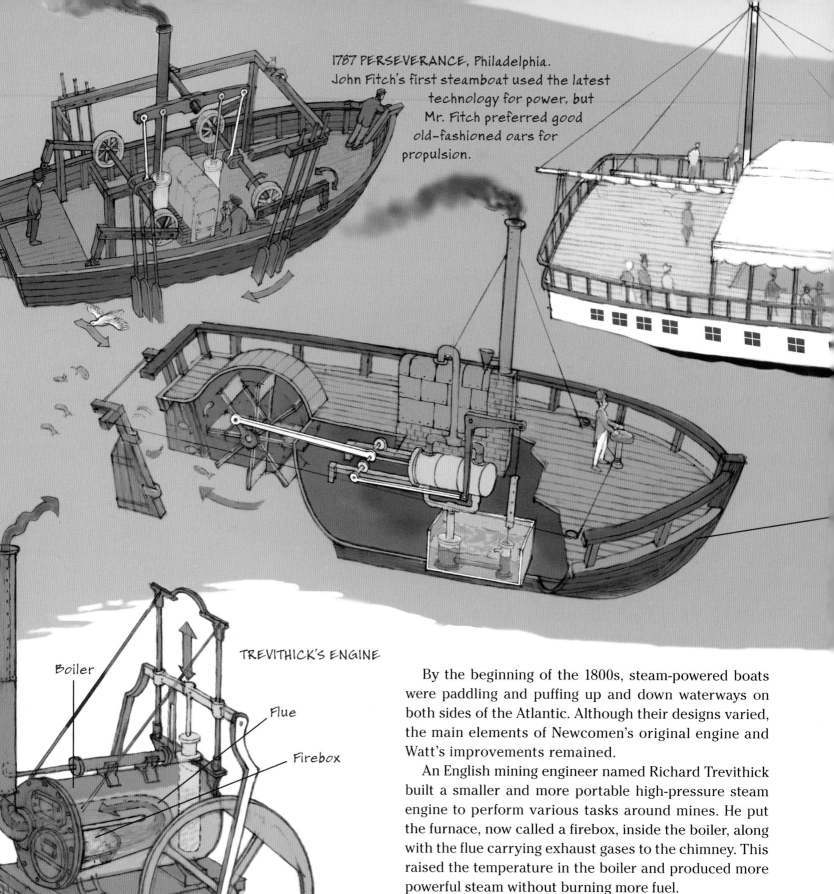

1787 PERSEVERANCE, Philadelphia. John Fitch's first steamboat used the latest technology for power, but Mr. Fitch preferred good old-fashioned oars for propulsion.

TREVITHICK'S ENGINE

Boiler

Flue

Firebox

By the beginning of the 1800s, steam-powered boats were paddling and puffing up and down waterways on both sides of the Atlantic. Although their designs varied, the main elements of Newcomen's original engine and Watt's improvements remained.

An English mining engineer named Richard Trevithick built a smaller and more portable high-pressure steam engine to perform various tasks around mines. He put the furnace, now called a firebox, inside the boiler, along with the flue carrying exhaust gases to the chimney. This raised the temperature in the boiler and produced more powerful steam without burning more fuel.

14

1807 NORTH RIVER STEAMBOAT,
also called CLERMONT, New York.
Robert Fulton built the second successful
steamboat (after PERSEVERANCE) to
carry passengers from New York to Albany.
The engine was built in England by Boulton
and Watt and shipped to the United States.

1803 CHARLOTTE DUNDAS, Scotland.
Designed by William Symington to
tow barges up and down canals.
Power was provided by a horizontal
steam engine connected to a
crank that turned a paddle wheel.

1805 ORUKTOR AMPHIBOLOS,
Philadelphia. A steam-powered
amphibious vehicle designed
by Oliver Evans for
dredging the
Delaware River.

Around 1804, wheels were attached to Trevithick's
engines so they could move themselves around. Although
these wheeled steam engines were smaller, they were still
too heavy for ordinary roads, so they were run on iron
rails like those used by miners for moving carts of coal. It
wasn't long before these locomotives and the cars they
pulled made their way out of the mines and were carrying
people as well as freight around the country.

1818 SAVANNAH,
United States, 98 feet

The paddles
of SAVANNAH's
wheels were tied
together by chains
so they could be
folded away in
rough seas.

SAVANNAH
had twin boilers
and a stack
with an angled
top that could
be rotated into
the direction
of the wind.

The growing success of steam engines on inland waterways was not lost on the owners of ocean-going ships. While they still couldn't guarantee that an ocean voyage would be pleasant, with this machinery they could at least promise to get it over with as quickly as possible.

A 98-foot-long wooden ship called *Savannah* was the first ocean-going vessel to add steam power to its complement of sails. In 1819 the ship made its one and only voyage back and forth across the Atlantic. Although *Savannah* relied much more on its sails than on its paddle wheels, within a little more than a decade the English-built *Curaçao* and the Canadian-built *Royal William* made the voyage primarily using steam.

1826 CURAÇAO, England, 128 feet

The engines in both CURAÇAO and ROYAL WILLIAM used two identical cylinders, each with a pair of levers to operate cranks on the paddle-wheel axle.

1831 ROYAL WILLIAM, Canada, 160 feet

1829 French engineer Marc Séguin improved the efficiency of high-pressure boilers by replacing the single flue pipe with a cluster of smaller pipes called fire tubes. This put the hot gases closer to the surrounding water, producing higher temperatures and more powerful steam. Railways on both sides of the Atlantic welcomed this innovation.

Propeller shaft

By the late 1830s, the Great Western Railway was carrying passengers by steam train from London to Bristol, on the west coast of England. In 1836, the company's chief engineer, Isambard Kingdom Brunel, suggested extending the journey all the way to the United States by steamship. *Great Western*, launched in 1838, was built to carry up to 200 passengers and crew. Because of the ship's length, the wooden hull was reinforced with iron straps to reduce bending. It could make the trip to New York in around 16 days, and return, with the help of the westerly winds in its sails, in about 13, setting speed records in both directions.

1843 GREAT BRITAIN, 322 feet
Capacity: almost 500, including crew
Iron hull
Propeller-driven, two twin-cylinder inclined engines,
single square boiler, and sails

Brunel's second ship, *Great Britain*, was almost a hundred feet longer and carried twice as many passengers. Brunel was in the middle of designing it when he became aware of two recent innovations: the iron hull and the screw propeller. Iron ships were not only stronger and lighter than wooden ships of the same size, but also resistant to rot and worms. And unlike paddle wheels, which tended to lift in and out of the water as the ship rolled from side to side, a propeller generally remained below the waterline. He then made two more improvements. He added an inner bottom above the outer bottom to provide extra protection should the ship run aground, and he divided the hull into several watertight compartments, an idea introduced by Chinese shipbuilders hundreds of years earlier. Even if one of the compartments filled with water, the ship would remain afloat.

1838 GREAT WESTERN, 235 feet
Capacity: 200, including crew
Oak hull with iron straps
two paddle wheels, two side-lever engines, four boilers, and sails

19

Buoyed by the success of his first two ships, in 1854 Brunel started work on his most ambitious vessel, *Great Eastern*. At almost 700 feet long and 82 feet wide, it was built to carry 4,000 passengers from England to India or Australia without stopping along the way for fuel or food. Instead of a single hull with a double bottom, *Great Eastern* had two hulls, one inside the other about 30 inches apart, and 19 watertight compartments. Four engines turned two 56-foot-diameter paddle wheels while a separate four-cylinder engine powered the 24-foot-diameter screw propeller. Six masts and auxiliary sails were also available.

Everything about *Great Eastern* was big—except for its success as a passenger ship. After suffering one catastrophe after another, it was taken out of service after only five years and seemed destined for an early visit to the scrapyard. But in 1866, thanks to its vast interior space, *Great Eastern* was put to work carrying and helping lay the first successful transatlantic telegraph cable, between Nova Scotia and Ireland.

Inner plates

Outer plates

Propeller shaft

Blue Riband Ships
and When They Held the Title

BALTIC, 282 feet,
1851–1856

PERSIA, 398 feet,
1856–1863

SCOTIA, 400 feet,
1863–1872

ADRIATIC, 452 feet,
1872–1875

Cross section of the double hull of GREAT EASTERN

Since *Great Eastern*'s size would remain unmatched for almost 50 years, competition between ships focused instead on speed. To help lure both passengers and government mail contracts, the liner completing the fastest crossing of the Atlantic was now recognized with an informal honor called the Blue Riband. The award was formalized in 1910, and beginning in 1935, a four-foot-high trophy was presented to the ship with the fastest crossing in the more difficult westbound direction.

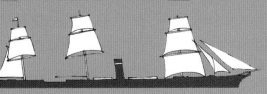

GERMANIC, 455 feet,
1875, 1877-1882

CITY OF BERLIN, 489 feet,
1875

BRITANNIC, 468 feet,
1876

Low-pressure cylinder

High-pressure cylinder

The Scotch boiler was similar to the fire-tube boilers used in railway locomotives, but much larger. All but one of SERVIA's seven boilers had three furnaces at each end.

Instead of using one big cylinder, compound engines used smaller cylinders of two different diameters. Steam at high pressure first passed through the smallest cylinder, driving its piston; then, with its power reduced, the same steam was piped into one or two larger cylinders to drive those pistons. The steam was doing twice as much work without using twice as much fuel. By the 1860s, shipbuilders began installing compound engines to meet the growing demand for power.

1881 SERVIA, 515 feet

One ship that wasn't quite fast enough to take the Blue Riband was launched by the Cunard Steamship Company in 1881. *Servia*, with its steel hull and efficient power plant, is considered to be the first modern ocean liner. Since steel is stronger than iron, the hull plates could be thinner. This reduced the ship's overall weight and saved fuel without sacrificing safety. Power was produced by a far more efficient steam engine called a compound engine, and the steam itself was produced more efficiently by using the latest fire-tube boilers, called Scotch boilers.

Servia's 1,500 passengers and crew also enjoyed the advantages of an Edison electric lighting system. Safer and more convenient than candles and oil lamps, incandescent bulbs illuminated the public spaces and the engine room. The generator that produced the electricity was powered by a small steam engine.

ALASKA, 520 feet, 1882-1883

OREGON, 521 feet, 1884

ETURIA, 519 feet, 1885, 1888

UMBRIA, 519 feet, 1887

CITY OF PARIS, 560 feet, 1889, 1892

MAJESTIC, 582 feet, 1889

CAMPANIA, 622 feet, 1893-1894

Servia was the second-biggest ship in the world, after *Great Eastern*, and in the years following its launch, ship lengths gradually increased, as did the sizes of their engines. The Blue Riband–holders *Majestic* and its running mate, *Teutonic*, were 582 feet long. Both ships were powered by a pair of screw propellers, each one driven by a massive triple-expansion engine.

Determined to recapture the Blue Riband, Cunard launched *Lucania* and its running mate, *Campania*, in 1892 and 1893, respectively. At 622 feet long, they were the largest, fastest, and most luxurious ships afloat—at least for the next five years, until 1897, when the German liner *Kaiser Wilhelm der Grosse* surpassed them.

While wealthy travelers were being wooed with exotic wood paneling, velvet drapes, and richly-upholstered armchairs, more and more of a ship's profits were coming from the lower fares of immigrants to North America. Of the 2,000 passengers on both *Campania* and *Lucania*, 600 were in first class, 400 in second class, and 1,000 in third class, also called steerage. Cunard assured steerage customers that their accommodations were "far in advance of that usually provided."

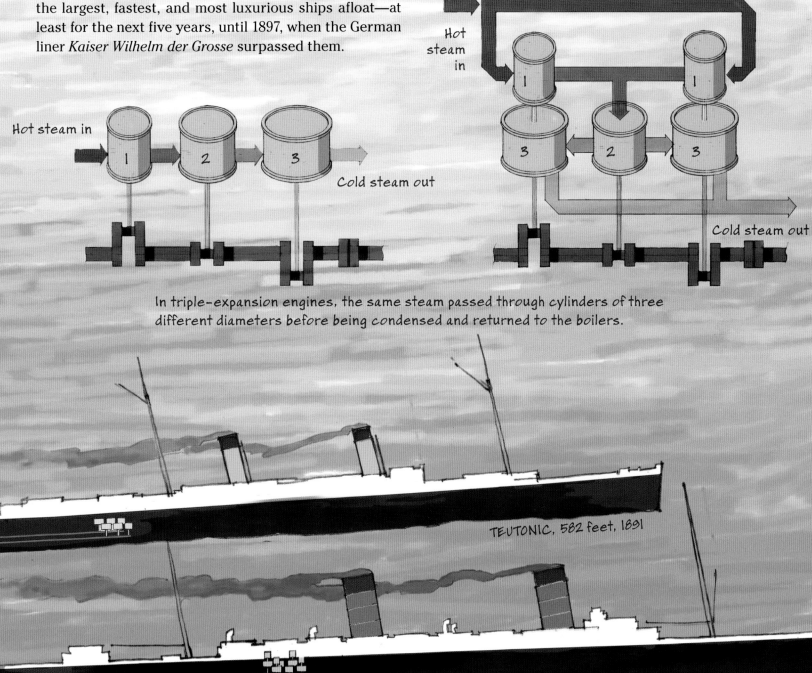

In triple-expansion engines, the same steam passed through cylinders of three different diameters before being condensed and returned to the boilers.

TEUTONIC, 582 feet, 1891

LUCANIA, 622 feet, 1894

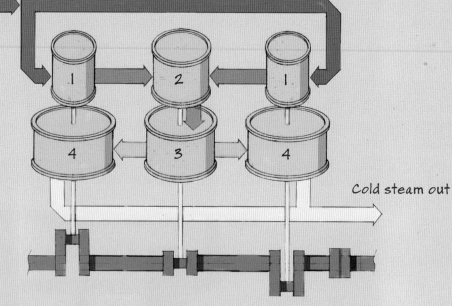

Hot steam in

Cold steam out

In quadruple-expansion engines the same steam passed through cylinders of four different diameters before being condensed and returned to the boilers.

NEW YORK

By 1894, forty-one years after the US-built ship *Baltic* took the Blue Riband, a much larger vessel was under construction in Philadelphia. Although *Saint Louis*, despite having the latest quadruple-expansion engines, was unable to repeat that earlier triumph, its launch inspired a journey that would culminate with the fastest ocean liner ever built and another American Blue Riband.

2

ON NOVEMBER 12, 1894, Mr. and Mrs. William Warren Gibbs took their family, including eight-year-old William Francis and six-year-old Frederic Herbert, to Cramp Shipyard to watch the launch of *Saint Louis*. The ship was bigger than anything young Willie Gibbs had ever seen. During summer vacations on the New Jersey shore, the sight of steamships gliding along the horizon had stirred his imagination. But watching and hearing one up close as it rumbled down the slipway and into the Delaware River was overwhelming.

From that moment on, William Francis began teaching himself how ships were designed, how they were built, and how they worked. By the age of twelve, he was devouring all the technical journals and books he could get his hands on. The more details, the better. Later, as a student at Harvard, he would often retreat to his room to study the plans of British battleships, drawing the changes he felt would improve their layout, speed, and safety.

In November of 1907, William Francis played hooky from Harvard so he could travel to England with his brother, Frederic. It wasn't their destination that mattered, however, but how they got there. The eastbound crossing was made on Cunard's Blue Riband ocean liner *Lusitania*, and they returned a few days later on the maiden voyage of *Lusitania*'s running mate, *Mauretania*, which would capture the fastest-crossing honor two years later. At almost 800 feet long, these were the largest ships afloat. Both owed their speed to four screw propellers driven by a new power source: Parsons turbines.

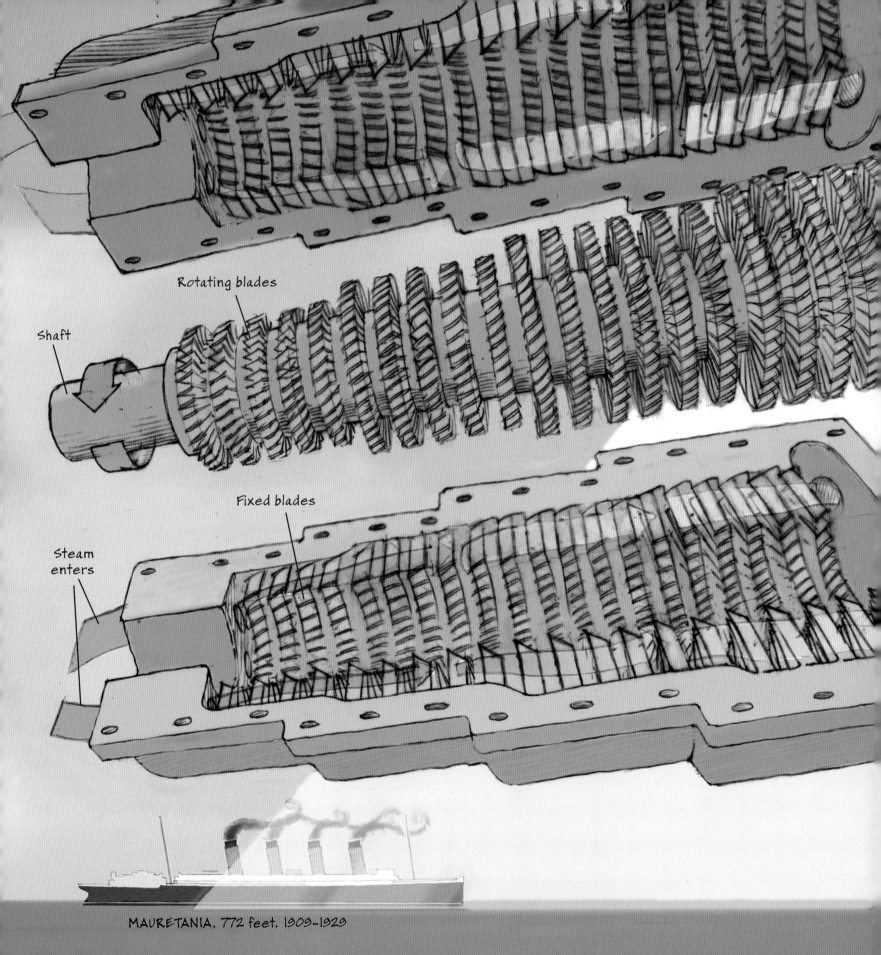

Rotating blades

Shaft

Fixed blades

Steam
enters

MAURETANIA, 772 feet, 1909-1929

32

Upper casing

Steam leaves

Lower casing

A Parsons turbine had two main parts: a stationary outer casing and a rotating inner shaft, each lined with rings of steel blades arranged in an alternating sequence. As steam passed between the fixed blades on the casing, it was directed against the rotating blades on the shaft, causing it to turn. Where the steam entered the turbine and its pressure was highest, the blades were relatively short. As the steam expanded through the turbine, its pressure dropped, so taller blades were needed.

An English engineer named Charles Algernon Parsons originally developed his steam turbines in the 1880s to power electrical generators, but then realized their usefulness in ships' engine rooms, where space and efficiency were at a premium. In addition to being smaller than piston engines, turbines could be directly connected to the propeller shaft, reducing the number of moving parts and simplifying maintenance.

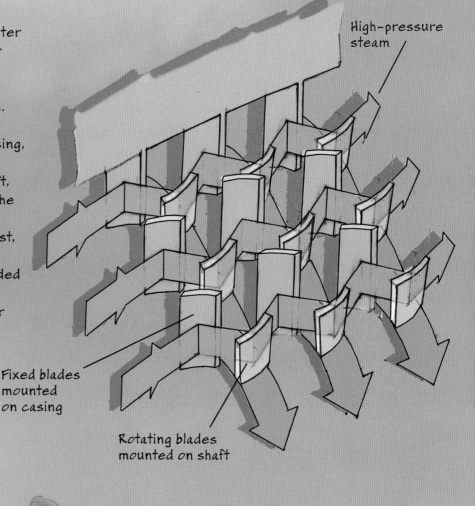

High-pressure steam

Fixed blades mounted on casing

Rotating blades mounted on shaft

LUSITANIA, 787 feet, 1907-1909

Boilers

Turbines

A year after completing his formal education, William Gibbs began designing his own superliner. Drawing on everything he had taught himself, he sketched out the longest, fastest, and most technically advanced passenger ship afloat.

While Willie drew, Frederic helped develop a business plan. It called for two identical ships to maintain a biweekly schedule between Europe and a brand-new terminal in Montauk, Long Island. In 1916, financier J. P. Morgan Jr. was so impressed by their efforts that he agreed to back the venture. The brothers set up shop in New York City and hired a small staff to turn their idea into a reality.

Unfortunately, things in Europe were not as rosy as they were in New York. The First World War had been raging for two years. The sinking of *Lusitania* in 1915 and the increasing threat of enemy U-boats lurking below the waves did little to encourage the sailing of large passenger ships across the Atlantic. Morgan halted the project and William Francis's dream became a casualty of the war while it was still on the drawing board.

In 1917 the German navy began sinking ships—including American ships—caught supplying Great Britain and its allies. The United States responded by declaring war on Germany and seizing the 950-foot-long luxury liner *Vaterland*, which had been docked in Hoboken, New Jersey, for safekeeping since 1914. The largest ship in the world and the pride of the Hamburg America Line was unceremoniously stripped of her lavish interiors and converted into an American troop carrier renamed *Leviathan*.

When the ship was finally released from these troop-carrying duties in December 1919, the Gibbs brothers were hired to study the ship for possible restoration. Since its German builders refused to provide blueprints to guide the work, the brothers enlisted a hundred draftsmen, who began by measuring every square inch of the ship, from the inside out. After two years of work, a new set of plans and specifications was ready. The brothers were then hired by the American transatlantic shipping company United States Lines to bring *Leviathan* back to its former splendor, but this time as an American luxury liner.

During the overhaul, *Leviathan*'s furnaces were converted to burn oil instead of coal. Ton for ton, oil produced twice as much energy. It was also cleaner and far less cumbersome to handle. And unlike coal, it could be stored wherever space was available and pumped to where it was needed.

Leviathan's maiden voyage created a lot of good publicity for the Gibbs brothers and United States Lines, but because the postwar economy was still uncertain, William Francis's dream ship remained on the drawing board.

The steam for LEVIATHAN's turbines was produced by a new type of boiler called a water-tube boiler. Unlike Scotch boilers, in which a cluster of pipes carried hot gases through a tank full of water, in water-tube boilers the pipes carried the water through the hot gases of the furnace, resulting in hotter and dryer steam.

Steam out

Water in

MALOLO, 582 feet, 1926

In 1926 the Gibbs brothers were back at Cramp Shipyard in Philadelphia, where as children they'd seen the launch of *Saint Louis*, for the launch of their first brand-new passenger liner, the 582-foot-long *Malolo*. A year later, during sea trials off the island of Nantucket, a Norwegian freighter suddenly emerged from a fog bank and tore a 14-foot-high gash in the side of *Malolo*'s hull. Fortunately, the ship was built with 12 watertight compartments and only two of them were flooded. Along with an extra 7,000 tons of New England seawater, *Malolo* had to be towed to New York for repairs. While not exactly the test William Francis had anticipated, the experience contributed to what would become a lifelong commitment to putting safety ahead of cost.

In 1930 the brothers were hired to design and build a small fleet of ships, each around 500 feet long, to carry cargo and passengers between New York and Los Angeles through the Panama Canal. To increase speed, reduce fuel consumption, and save valuable cargo space, *Santa Rosa, Santa Paula, Santa Elena,* and *Santa Lucia* were equipped with the latest American-made turbines, boilers, and reduction gears.

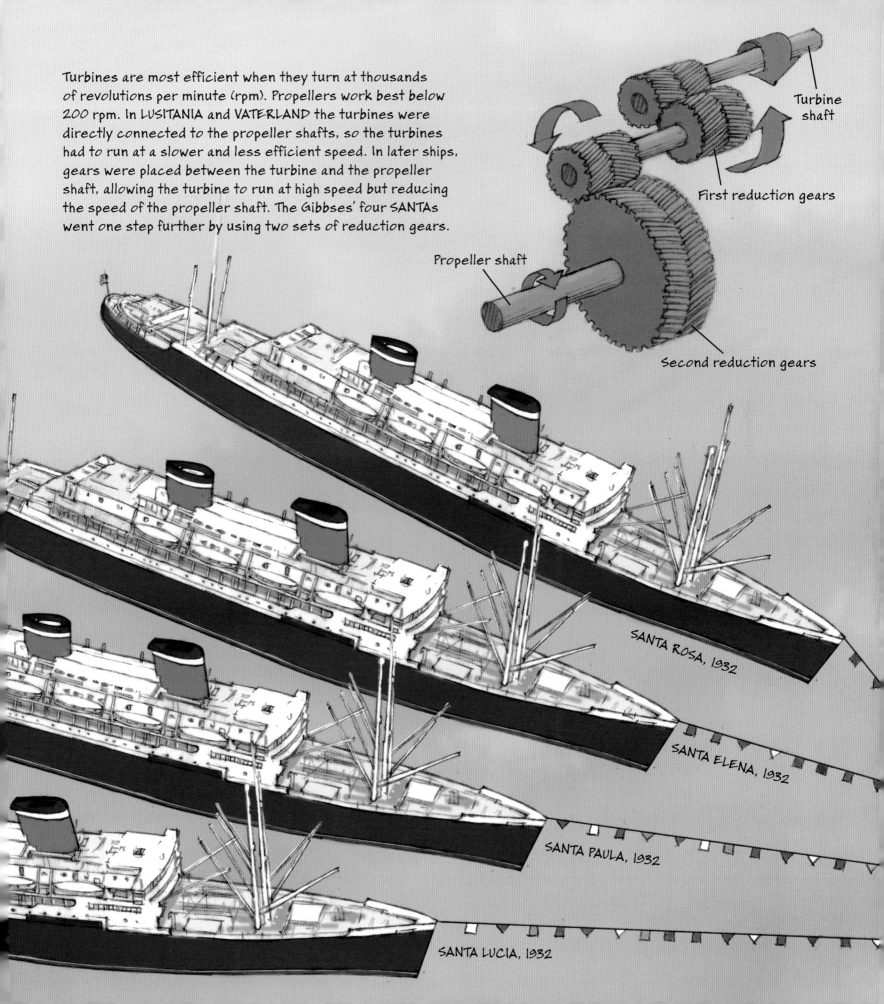

Turbines are most efficient when they turn at thousands of revolutions per minute (rpm). Propellers work best below 200 rpm. In LUSITANIA and VATERLAND the turbines were directly connected to the propeller shafts, so the turbines had to run at a slower and less efficient speed. In later ships, gears were placed between the turbine and the propeller shaft, allowing the turbine to run at high speed but reducing the speed of the propeller shaft. The Gibbses' four SANTAs went one step further by using two sets of reduction gears.

Turbine shaft

First reduction gears

Propeller shaft

Second reduction gears

SANTA ROSA, 1932

SANTA ELENA, 1932

SANTA PAULA, 1932

SANTA LUCIA, 1932

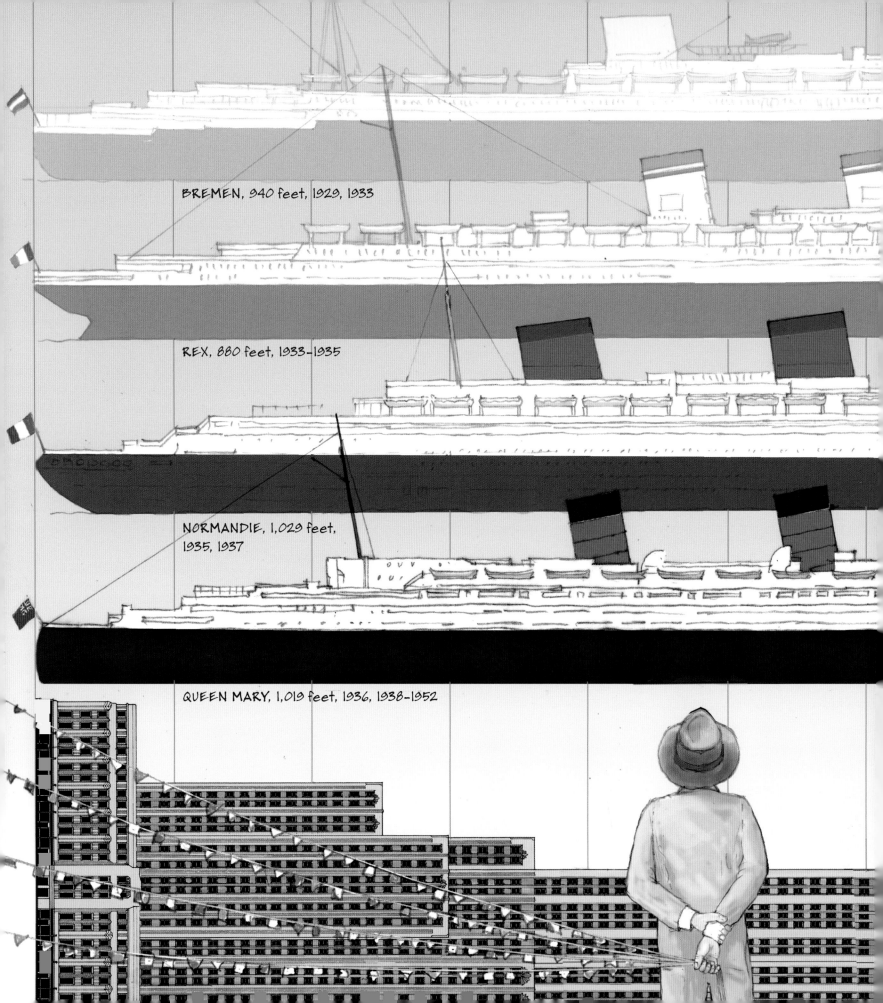

BREMEN, 940 feet, 1929, 1933

REX, 880 feet, 1933-1935

NORMANDIE, 1,029 feet,
1935, 1937

QUEEN MARY, 1,019 feet, 1936, 1938-1952

But while his business grew, William Francis's super-liner remained a dream. He could only watch in frustration as the Blue Riband passed from one large European vessel to another. Germany's *Bremen* was defeated by Italy's *Rex*. France's *Normandie*, driven by electric motors, then knocked off *Rex*. Britain's *Queen Mary* topped *Normandie*, only to have *Normandie* reclaim the honor. Finally, in 1938, *Queen Mary* began a reign that would last for 14 years.

Although a willingness to build big and fast eluded the American shipping industry, it was alive and well in the field of architecture. When completed in 1931, the Empire State Building became the tallest man-made structure in the world—and set a speed record with a construction time of just under 13 months.

1931, EMPIRE STATE BUILDING, 1,250 feet

AMERICA, 723 feet, 1939

The Gibbs brothers' reputation was also reaching new heights during the 1930s. When the United States Navy began updating its aging fleet, they hired the brothers' firm to oversee the building of 16 new destroyers. Instead of building these ships piece by piece in the traditional way, they were constructed from large preassembled sections called subassemblies. Most of these subassemblies were built upside down to save time and to avoid the dangers of welding overhead. Pleased with the finished products, the Navy showed its gratitude over the next 10 years by awarding the company contracts for almost 7,000 more ships, including Liberty ships, minesweepers, destroyer escorts, and landing craft.

In 1936, United States Lines commissioned the Gibbses' firm to design a new medium-sized passenger liner. The 723-foot-long *America* was launched in 1939 and completed in 1940. The ship was originally intended for the North Atlantic route, but with the outbreak of World War II in Europe, its travels were limited to the east coast of the United States and to the Caribbean. One year later, in 1941, the vessel was requisitioned by the government to serve as a troop carrier for the duration of the war.

By 1946 *America* was finally carrying paying passengers across the Atlantic. A year later *Queen Mary*, also freed from troop-carrying duties, would be back on its Blue Riband throne. With competition heating up, United States Lines approached Gibbs about building another liner. What they asked for was something a little larger than *America*. What they eventually got was the vision that had been evolving in Gibbs's mind for 30 years.

Like his very first design, the ship was to be around 1,000 feet long and just over 100 feet wide, making it the largest passenger liner ever built in the United States. It would be equipped with an engine and boiler combination more powerful than anything in commercial shipping. Frederic Gibbs's initial estimate for the ship came in at around $50 million, which was twice as much as United States Lines could afford. Like all large passenger liners, it would need government support.

Overall length 990 feet

WARTIME CAPACITY

In peacetime, this luxury liner would compete with the *Queen*s and carry around 2,000 passengers in style and comfort. In time of war, Design 12201, as it was known in the office, could quickly be adapted to ferry 14,000 soldiers up to 10,000 miles at high speed without stopping. In order to be able to reach Asia and the Pacific, the ship was just small enough to pass through the Panama Canal.

Among the ship's safety features were 20 watertight compartments and a double hull, separate enclosed engine and boiler rooms, fireproof material throughout, and the elimination of all but a few bits of wood. Although these and other features would cause the final cost to exceed $75 million, Gibbs's proposal was eventually accepted. In its dual roles, this one vessel would give the country and the company an inspiring flagship, *America,* a running mate, and *Queen Mary* heartburn.

Traveling through the Panama Canal was a tight fit. The locks were 1,000 feet in length, and the width was 110 feet, allowing the ship 4 feet of clearance on each side. The locks' depth was 42.5 feet, just 10 feet beneath the hull.

A Panama Canal lock

PEACETIME CAPACITY

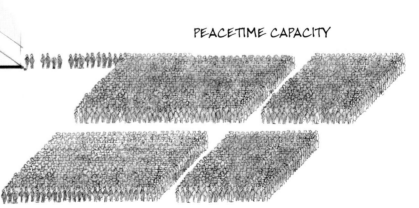

The speed of any ship depends on a combination of power, shape, and weight. To keep this ship as light as possible, much of the superstructure (everything above the steel hull) was to be built of aluminum, which, while not as strong as steel, is about 60 percent lighter.

Design 12201 would be driven by four screw propellers, each one turned by a pair of turbines producing 60,000 horsepower. Steam superheated in the boilers to almost 1,000 degrees would travel first to high-pressure turbines spinning their blades at 5,000 rpm, then to larger low-pressure turbines spinning their blades at 3,500 rpm. Reduction gears converted the speed produced by the turbines to a much more useful 150 rpm at the propeller shaft.

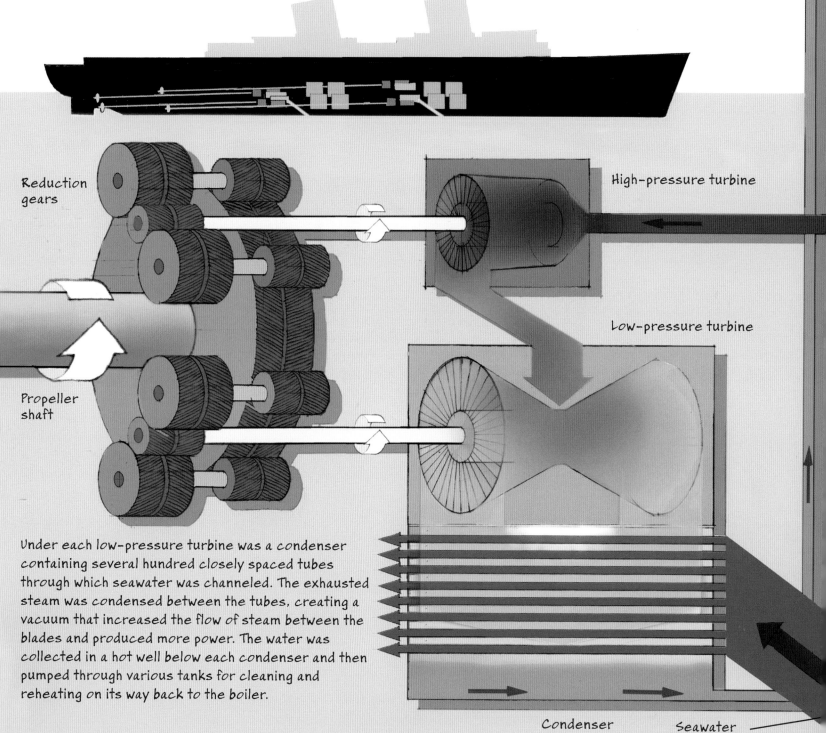

Reduction gears

High-pressure turbine

Low-pressure turbine

Propeller shaft

Under each low-pressure turbine was a condenser containing several hundred closely spaced tubes through which seawater was channeled. The exhausted steam was condensed between the tubes, creating a vacuum that increased the flow of steam between the blades and produced more power. The water was collected in a hot well below each condenser and then pumped through various tanks for cleaning and reheating on its way back to the boiler.

Condenser   Seawater

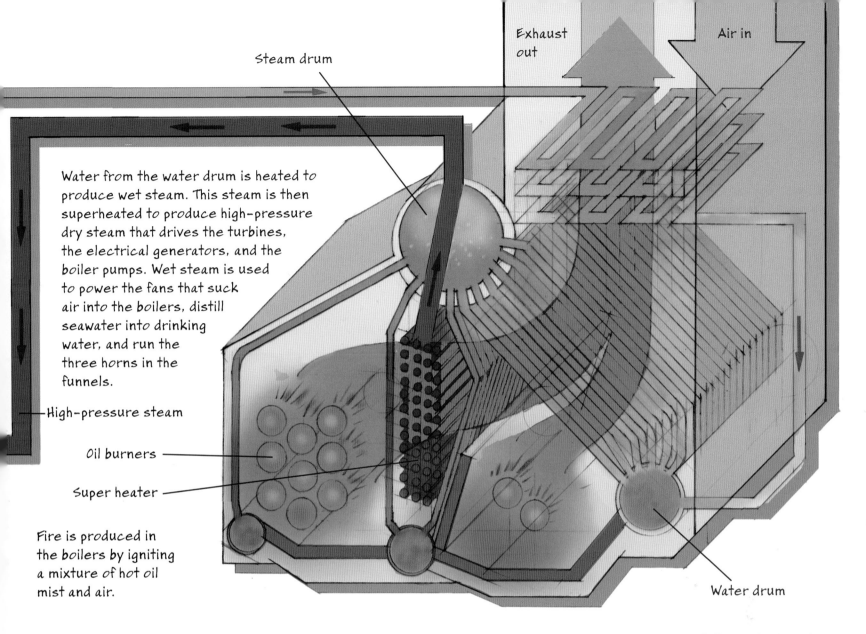

Steam drum

Exhaust out

Air in

Water from the water drum is heated to produce wet steam. This steam is then superheated to produce high-pressure dry steam that drives the turbines, the electrical generators, and the boiler pumps. Wet steam is used to power the fans that suck air into the boilers, distill seawater into drinking water, and run the three horns in the funnels.

High-pressure steam

Oil burners

Super heater

Fire is produced in the boilers by igniting a mixture of hot oil mist and air.

Water drum

To determine the most efficient shape for 12201's hull, a 20-foot-long wooden model was built based on Gibbs's specifications. After being equipped with various recording devices, the model was fastened beneath a movable gantry and towed down a long water-filled tank. Tests were performed at different speeds and under various wave conditions. The results were carefully studied, and between tests, the model was refined to improve its performance. When the engineers were confident they had the best shape possible, the curvature of the surface was painstakingly documented so it could be accurately reproduced when making patterns for the full-sized ship.

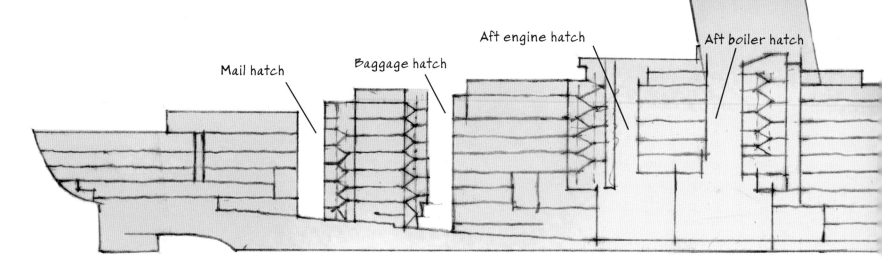

Mail hatch

Baggage hatch

Aft engine hatch

Aft boiler hatch

As the decks were being divided into rooms and corridors of various shapes and sizes, they were also being connected vertically by shafts and hatchways. The shafts would house staircases, including a couple of spirals, passenger and crew elevators, and even a few dumbwaiters for moving food between the ship's galleys and the upper decks. Of the eight large hatches, four were used for lowering cargo and mail to various storage areas and holds and four provided fresh air and ventilation to the engine and boiler rooms and housed the flues that would carry hot exhaust gases from the eight massive boilers to the funnels.

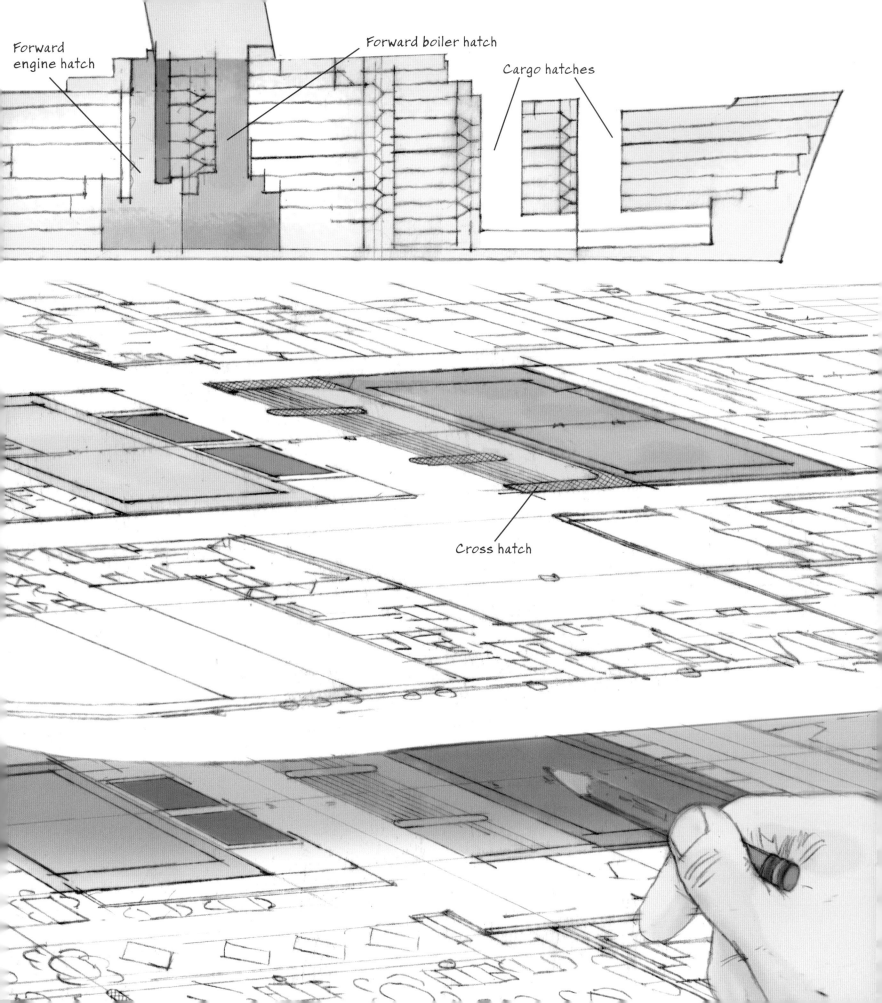

Forward engine hatch

Forward boiler hatch

Cargo hatches

Cross hatch

Random slices to show the changing profile of the hull
at different frames (lightly toasted)

Navigation Bridge Deck

Sports Deck

Sun Deck

Promenade Deck

Upper Deck

Main Deck

A Deck

B Deck

C Deck

D Deck

E Deck

The lowest deck (not shown)
is the bottom of the inner hull.

By 1949 an army of draftsmen had produced hundreds of plans documenting everything from structural steelwork and rivet placement to galley layouts and paint colors. Between the bidding process to decide which shipyard would actually build the ship and then construction itself, the number of plans would mushroom into thousands of blueprints. To help locate each piece of information on all the drawings, the length of the ship had been divided like a loaf of bread into 365 slices called frames. During construction, frame numbers would be painted on the walls and columns so the workers would know exactly where they were.

While the ship was being organized into frames, the Macaulay family was organizing itself into boxes. We were about to make our first big move—all 85 miles of it—north to the town of Bolton. My father went ahead to begin his new job while the rest of us lived temporarily with my grandparents. This process would repeat itself eight years later, although the distance to be covered would be significantly greater.

3

IN MAY 1949, Newport News Shipbuilding and Dry Dock Company in Newport News, Virginia, was chosen to build the new superliner. Construction would take place in one of their largest dry docks. Shipway No. 10 was 960 feet long by 128 feet wide. Its floor sat 35 feet below sea level. The open end was sealed by a temporary steel barrier called a caisson. When the shipway was pumped dry, the pressure of the James River against the caisson would keep it in place for as long as necessary.

Although the ship would slightly overhang both ends, the dry dock's depth would insure that its design below the waterline remained well hidden. This satisfied Gibbs, who was secretive about all the ship's details—but particularly those that might give away any clues as to its potential speed.

Like most of Gibbs's ships for the navy, Hull 488, as it was called, was to be constructed almost entirely of sub-assemblies—over 180,000 of them. Steel plates were cut to size, shaped, and assembled into sections in the work area adjacent to Shipway No. 10 and then hoisted into place. The contract called for the dry-dock portion of the ship's construction to be completed in 18 months. To maintain the demanding schedule, the building of the subassemblies had to be carefully orchestrated so they would be ready exactly when needed.

On February 8, 1950, both Gibbs brothers joined a group of shipyard officials for the "laying of the keel," the traditional placement of the first piece of the ship's "back-bone." This section happened to be 108 feet long and weigh 55 tons. The most critical task (besides not drop-ping it on the spectators) was getting it perfectly aligned on the keel blocks, a five-foot-wide and five-foot-high wall of yellow pine that stretched down the middle of the ship-way. If this first subassembly was even slightly out of line, the rest of the ship could suffer, jeopardizing its speed and handling at sea. With the great weight hovering just a few inches above the blocks, shipwrights gently tugged and nudged it into position before it came to rest.

After the viewing party left, February 8 became a regular workday. In less than an hour the second section was lowered onto the keel block, establishing a pace of construction that would be maintained for the next year and a half. Having waited more than 30 years for this, William Francis traveled from New York almost every weekend to make sure the plans were being care-fully followed. No detail escaped his attention.

As soon as the first sections of keel were on the blocks, the bottom plates of the outer hull were laid parallel to it along both sides. These plates were welded end to end to form long strips called strakes. Where the strakes overlapped the keel and each other, they were fastened together with two or three rows of rivets. Each preassembled section of inner hull, complete with its cellular framework, was then lowered onto the bottom plates and welded into place.

The floor of the inner hull is also called the tank top because the space between it and the outer hull is used to store fuel oil and salt water.

Inner wall subassembly

Inner hull subassembly

Keel

Outer hull

Watertight bulkhead

Bilge keel

By mid-March the bottom of the double hull had reached the bilge, where it turned upward to form the walls. The inner wall subassemblies were lowered into position first, after which the plates of the outer wall were added. A pair of bladelike extensions known as bilge keels was then fastened to the bilge on each side of the hull. These were intended to reduce rolling from side to side when the ship was under way. The walls of the double hull were temporarily stabilized by a combination of beams and cables until the watertight bulkheads were installed.

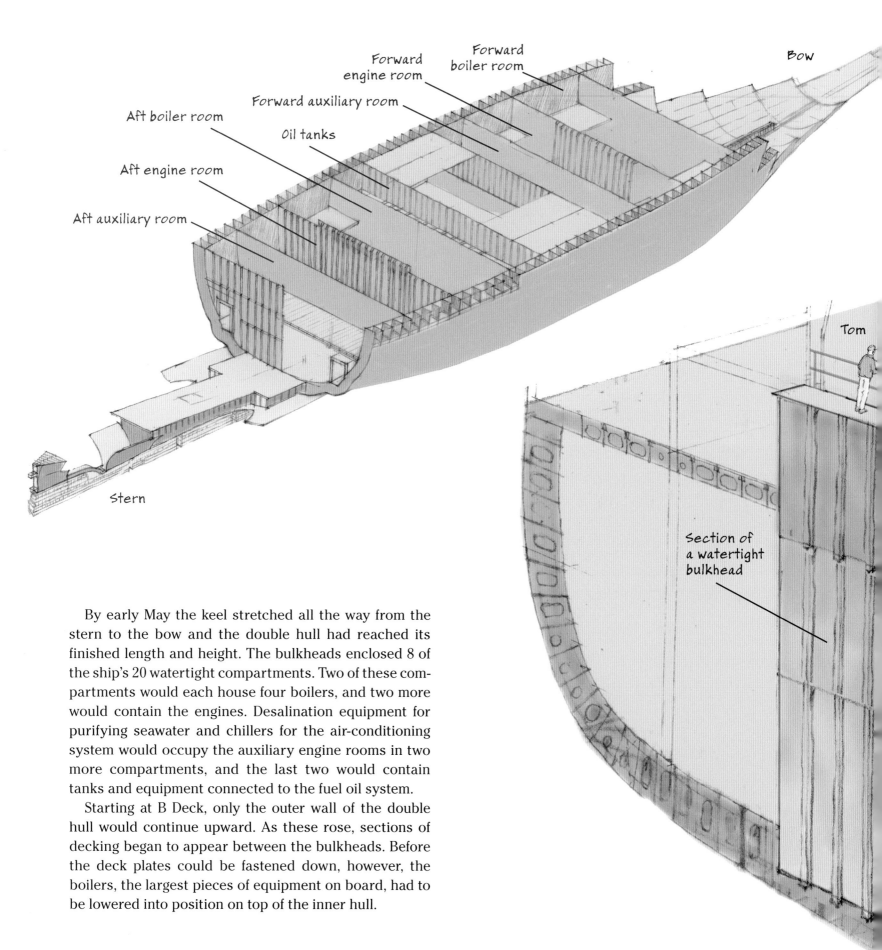

Forward boiler room

Forward engine room

Forward auxiliary room

Aft boiler room

Oil tanks

Aft engine room

Aft auxiliary room

Stern

Bow

Tom

Section of a watertight bulkhead

By early May the keel stretched all the way from the stern to the bow and the double hull had reached its finished length and height. The bulkheads enclosed 8 of the ship's 20 watertight compartments. Two of these compartments would each house four boilers, and two more would contain the engines. Desalination equipment for purifying seawater and chillers for the air-conditioning system would occupy the auxiliary engine rooms in two more compartments, and the last two would contain tanks and equipment connected to the fuel oil system.

Starting at B Deck, only the outer wall of the double hull would continue upward. As these rose, sections of decking began to appear between the bulkheads. Before the deck plates could be fastened down, however, the boilers, the largest pieces of equipment on board, had to be lowered into position on top of the inner hull.

Internal
structure
of a boiler

Dumbwaiters

Main Deck

Hank

A Deck

B Deck

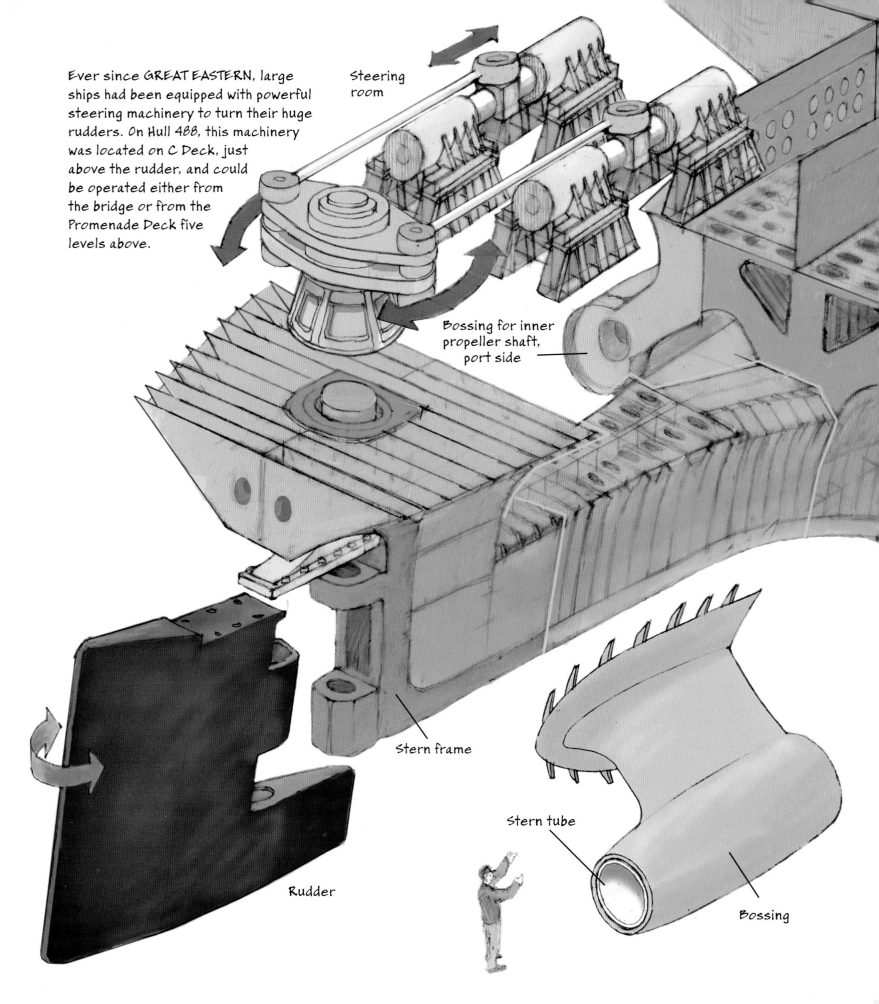

Ever since GREAT EASTERN, large ships had been equipped with powerful steering machinery to turn their huge rudders. On Hull 488, this machinery was located on C Deck, just above the rudder, and could be operated either from the bridge or from the Promenade Deck five levels above.

Steering room

Bossing for inner propeller shaft, port side

Stern frame

Rudder

Stern tube

Bossing

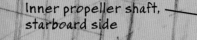

Inner propeller shaft, starboard side

Lignum vitae seal

Bossing

Last piece of the propeller shaft (tail shaft)

Outer propeller shaft, starboard side

At the stern, the hull below the waterline gradually tapered to direct the flow of water toward the propellers and against the sides of the rudder. In this portion of the ship, the spacing between the frames was reduced to strengthen the structure and minimize vibration caused by the propellers. A large casting called the stern frame was embedded in one of the subassemblies to support the rudder. Above the waterline, the hull widened and extended beyond the rudder to provide more usable deck space.

Inside the hull, portions of the propeller shafts were enclosed in watertight tunnels for safety. As the shafts passed through the hull, these tunnels were extended out into the water in streamlined bulges called bossings. At the ends of the bossings, the propeller shafts passed through the stern tube before emerging into the water. The space between the shaft and the stern tube was sealed with a very hard, self-lubricating wood called lignum vitae to minimize leakage.

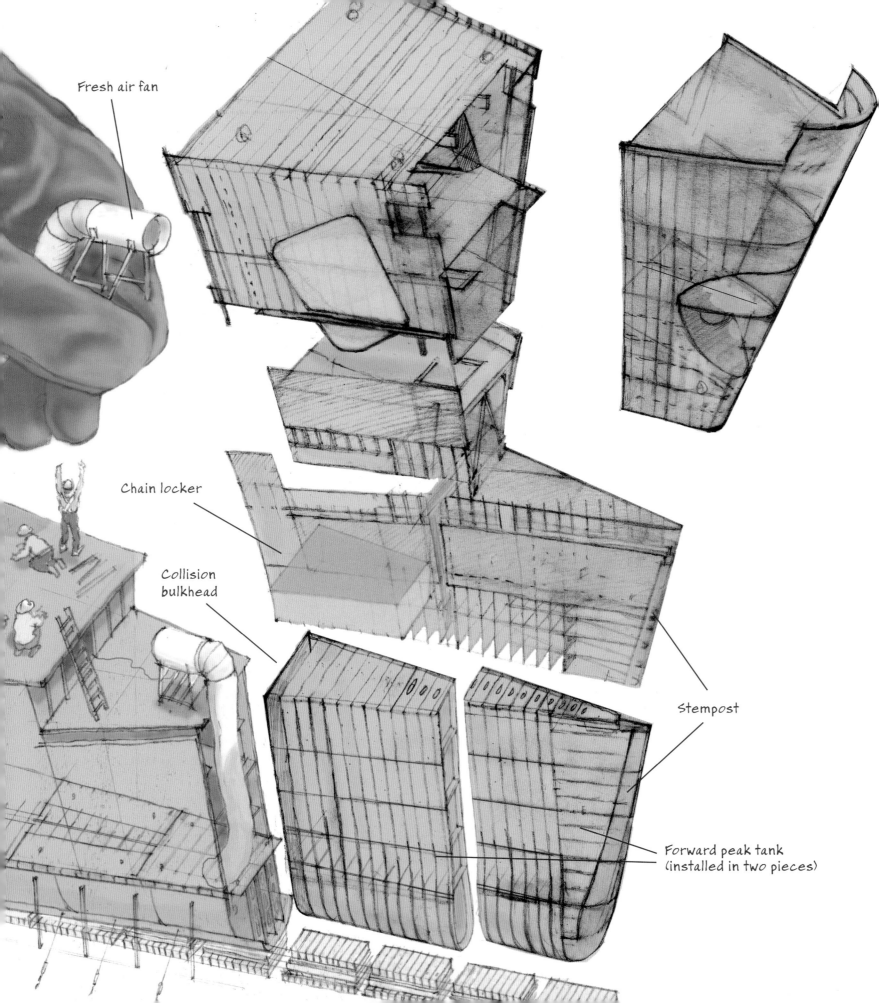

Fresh air fan

Chain locker

Collision
bulkhead

Stempost

Forward peak tank
(installed in two pieces)

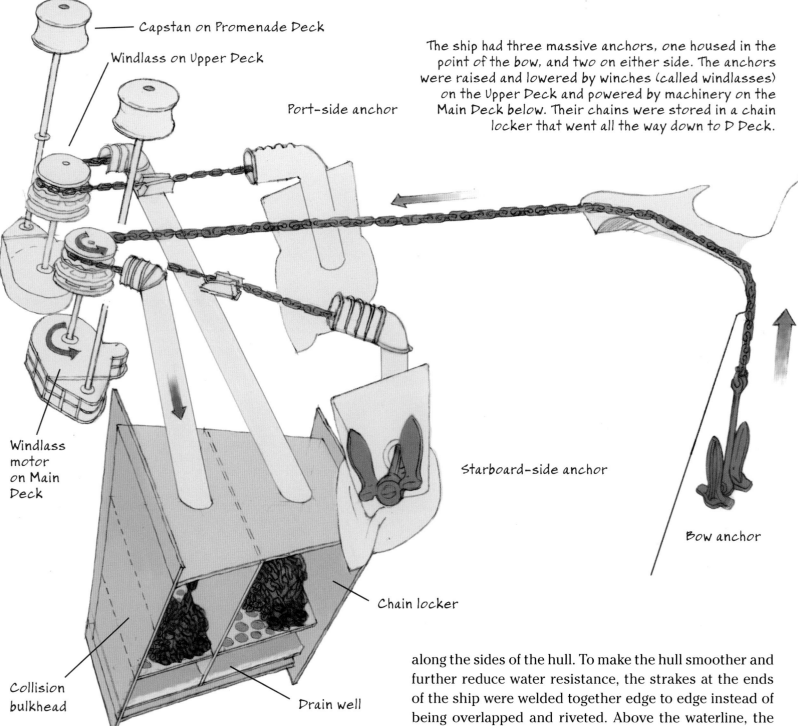

Capstan on Promenade Deck

Windlass on Upper Deck

Port-side anchor

The ship had three massive anchors, one housed in the point of the bow, and two on either side. The anchors were raised and lowered by winches (called windlasses) on the Upper Deck and powered by machinery on the Main Deck below. Their chains were stored in a chain locker that went all the way down to D Deck.

Windlass motor on Main Deck

Starboard-side anchor

Bow anchor

Collision bulkhead

Drain well

Chain locker

Like the stern, the bow was strengthened with closely spaced framing to withstand the North Atlantic's pounding waves. The front edge of the bow was reinforced along most of its height by a column of V- or U-shaped steel plates called the stempost. At the waterline, the stempost was just a few inches wide, but by the time it reached the keel it was six feet across. This bulge was created to push the water out of the way and direct it more efficiently along the sides of the hull. To make the hull smoother and further reduce water resistance, the strakes at the ends of the ship were welded together edge to edge instead of being overlapped and riveted. Above the waterline, the bow fanned out to provide space for work, storage, and crew quarters, as well as for the machinery that would raise and lower the ship's three anchors.

Resting on the keel between the stempost and the first watertight bulkhead, called the collision bulkhead, was a large tank known as the forward peak tank. This and a similar tank in the stern could be filled with seawater to reduce pitching, the tendency of the ship to dip and rise in rough seas.

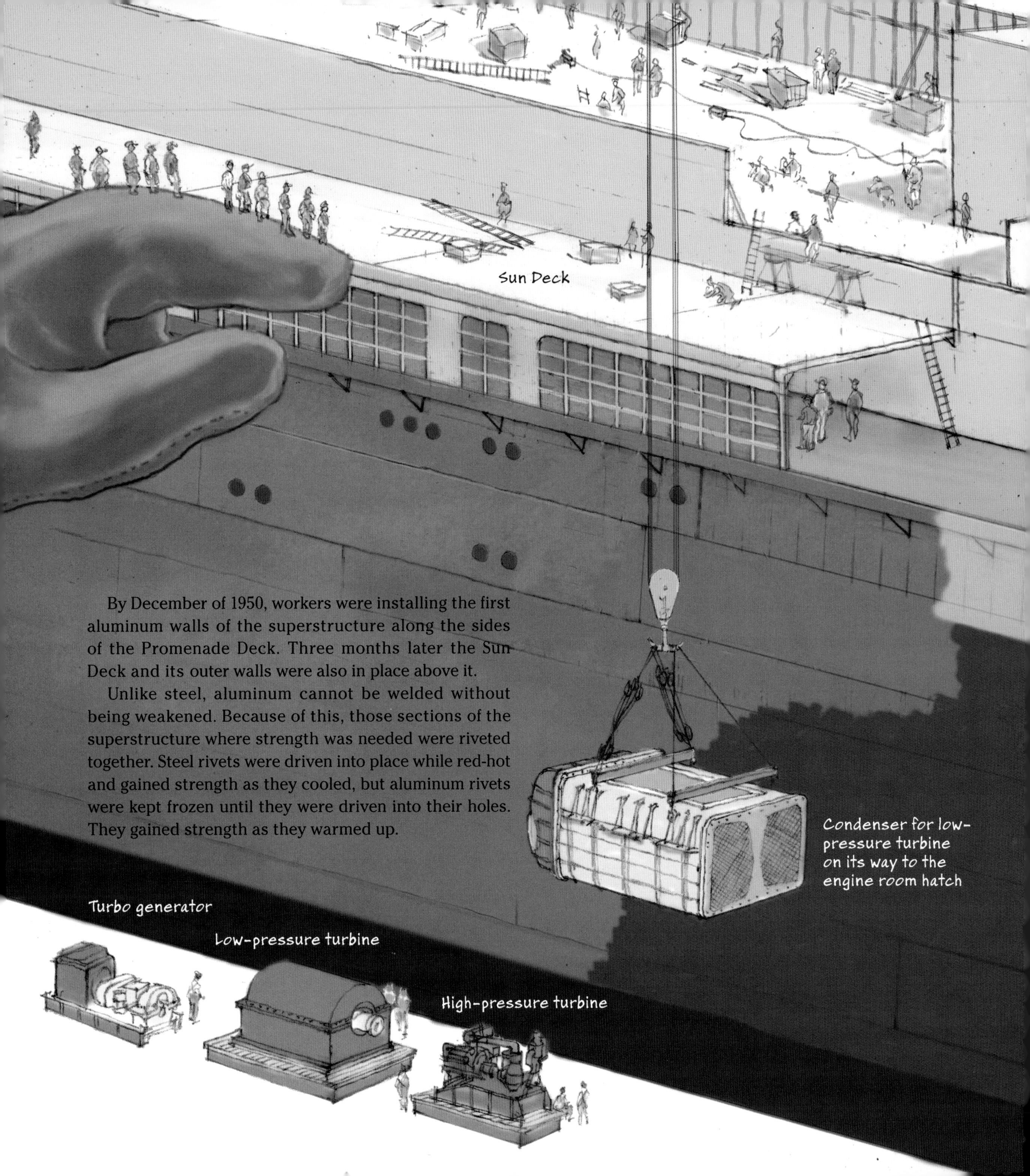

By December of 1950, workers were installing the first aluminum walls of the superstructure along the sides of the Promenade Deck. Three months later the Sun Deck and its outer walls were also in place above it.

Unlike steel, aluminum cannot be welded without being weakened. Because of this, those sections of the superstructure where strength was needed were riveted together. Steel rivets were driven into place while red-hot and gained strength as they cooled, but aluminum rivets were kept frozen until they were driven into their holes. They gained strength as they warmed up.

Sun Deck

Condenser for low-pressure turbine on its way to the engine room hatch

Turbo generator

Low-pressure turbine

High-pressure turbine

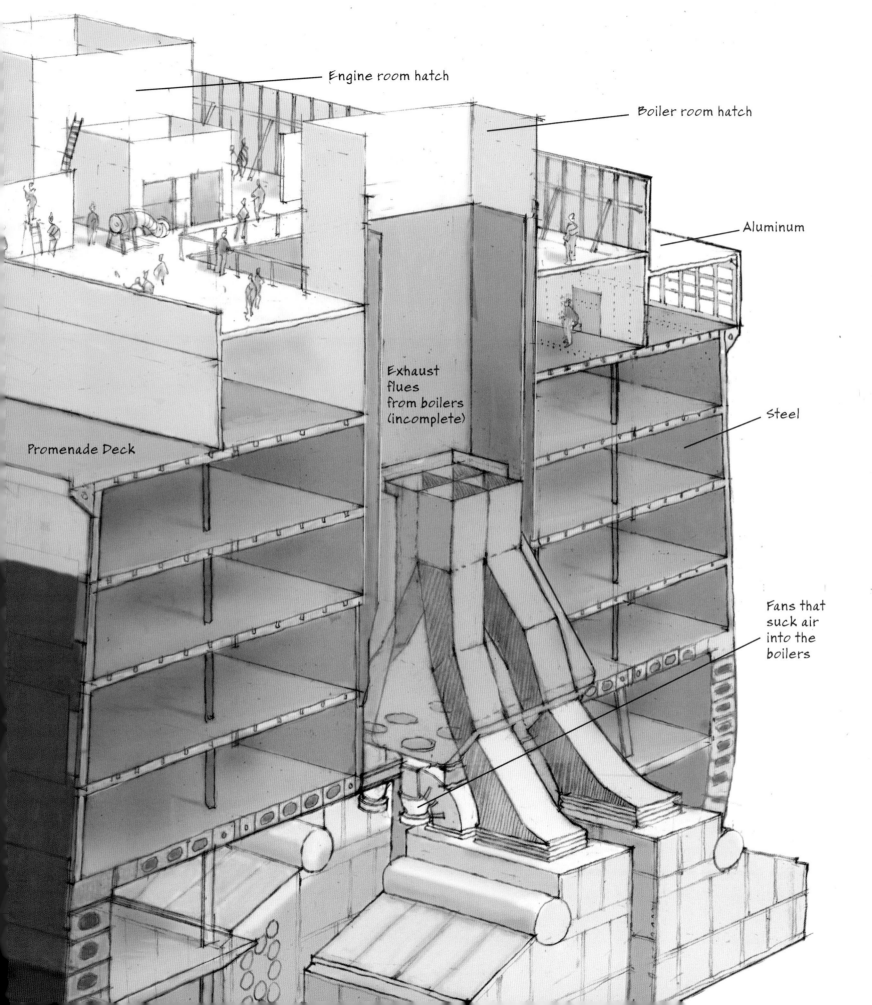

Engine room hatch

Boiler room hatch

Aluminum

Steel

Exhaust
flues
from boilers
(incomplete)

Promenade Deck

Fans that
suck air
into the
boilers

In the work area next to the dry dock, the huge, streamlined funnels that would make the ship immediately recognizable were nearing completion. Each was built of aluminum plates fastened to a mostly aluminum skeleton and capped by a rounded roof called a sampan. The complex curvature of the sampan required that many of the pieces be hammered into shape over specially made forms. The sloping fins at the rear of the sampans were a Gibbs trademark. For this ship, they had been put through wind-tunnel tests to make sure they would direct the exhaust and escaping soot away from passengers.

Beneath the hull, shipwrights on the floor of the dry dock were installing the propellers. The two forward propellers each had four blades, while the aft propellers were equipped with five blades to make them more effective in water that had already been churned up by the forward pair.

Each propeller started as a full-sized wooden model from which cement molds were made. Once the mold hardened and the wooden model had been removed, the empty space was filled with molten bronze. The finished castings were then painstakingly chipped and ground down to their exact shape to minimize cavitation—the tendency of air bubbles in the water to damage the surface of the propellers and reduce their efficiency.

Radar mast

In May the funnels were installed. Because of their size, each had to be lifted aboard in two pieces. Once these were in place, the forward king posts were positioned next to the cargo hatches. A pair of long booms hinged to each king post would be used to lower cargo into the holds far below. Inside the hatch at each deck level, a pair of drawbridges could be raised to let cargo pass up or down, or closed to provide additional storage space.

During construction, much of the wooden framework beneath the hull was replaced by a few large supports similar to the keel blocks. These would keep the ship from tipping while also making it easier for painters to reach the plating with their antifouling paint. This covering would prevent small sea creatures from attaching themselves to the hull and slowing the ship down. The only other supports appeared along the bilges as the hull narrowed toward the bow. They were a combination of timber posts, called shores, and steel tie rods.

By the third week of June, all the shoring and rods had been removed, leaving the ship supported entirely on the blocks.

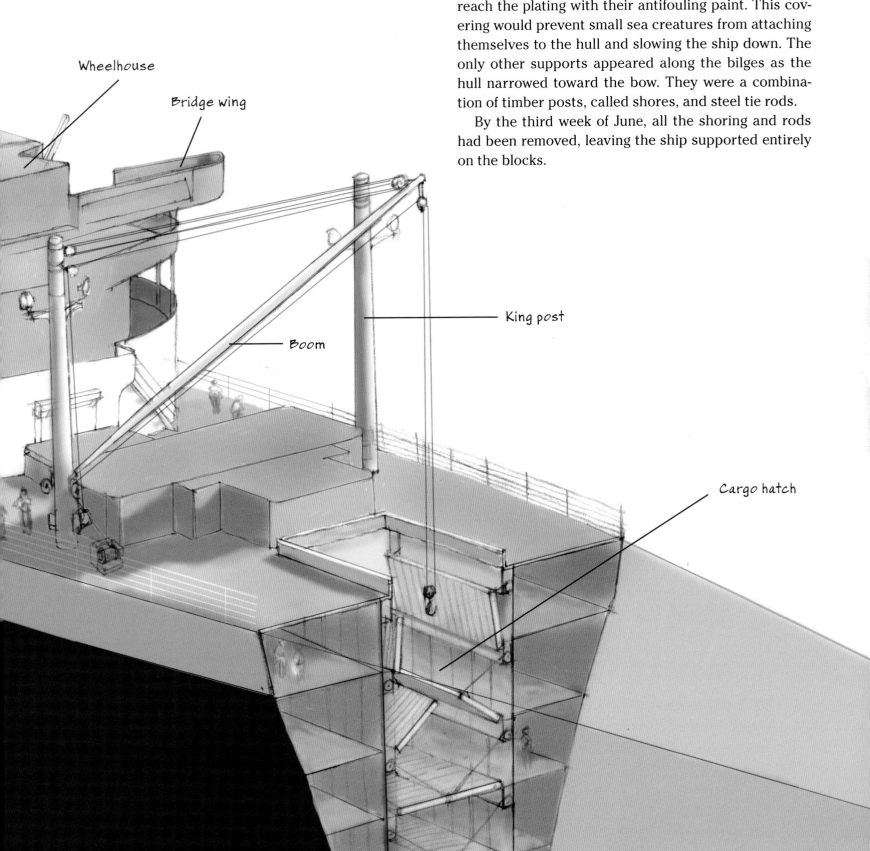

Wheelhouse

Bridge wing

King post

Boom

Cargo hatch

On the morning of June 22, 1951, the bottom of Hull 488 was given one last inspection, and at 4:30 that afternoon sluice gates in the side wall of the dry dock were opened. William Francis watched from the top of the caisson as the muddy waters of the James River began lapping against the sides of his masterpiece. Twelve hours later, the ship was afloat and connected to dry land by just a few sturdy ropes. When the water level in Shipway No. 10 matched that of the river, the caisson could be safely removed. As the water inside it was pumped out, the caisson began to float, breaking the seal that had existed for 18 months, after which a pair of tugboats towed it away.

By midday on June 23, thousands of people had gathered in the heat and humidity of Newport News to witness the ship's official christening. Preferring to avoid attention, Gibbs remained near the podium, but not on it. The presence of newsreel cameras and microphones from radio stations near and far reminded everyone that this was much more than a local achievement; this was a national achievement. Following the speeches and musical selections, the wife of the senator from Texas smashed a bottle of champagne against the ship's towering bow and officially named it *United States*. The crowd was still cheering and waving flags as eight carefully positioned tugboats began pulling the ship out into the river for the brief journey to the pier, where it would be fitted out.

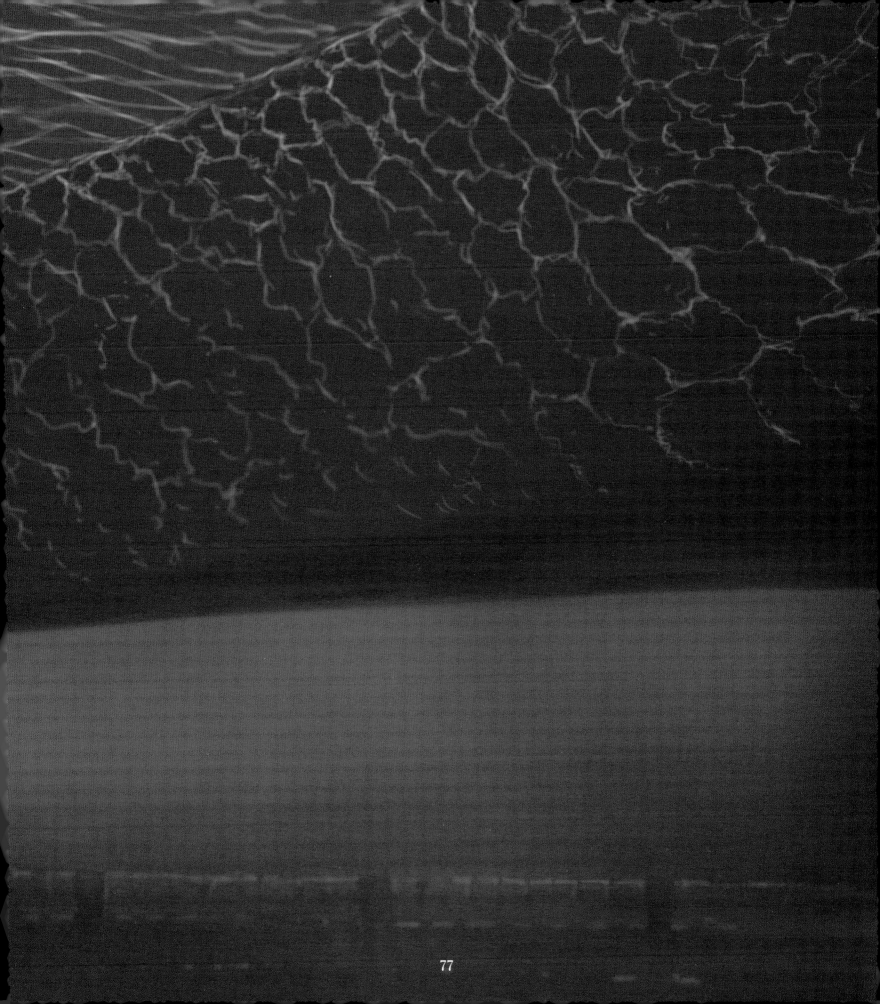

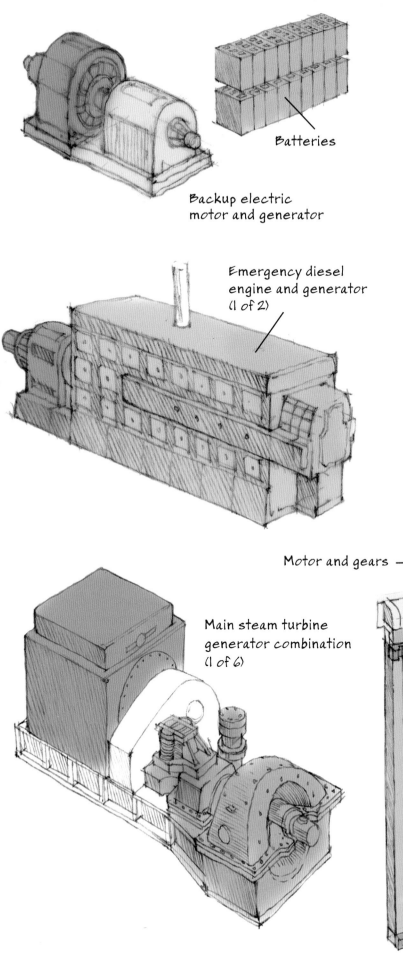

Batteries

Backup electric
motor and generator

Emergency diesel
engine and generator
(1 of 2)

Main steam turbine
generator combination
(1 of 6)

Project 12201 was designed to be the fastest passenger liner afloat, but it also had to be the safest. Gibbs was particularly concerned about the danger of fire at sea. For this reason, almost everything on the ship except passenger belongings was fireproof. The only wood he allowed belonged to a couple of grand pianos and a few chopping blocks in the galleys. To prevent the spread of a fire should one occur, the ship was divided into fire zones to contain any outbreak. These zones were enclosed between certain bulkheads which were sheathed in a nonflammable, asbestos-filled material called Marinite. All the decks were equipped with fire hydrants and hoses, and special pumps would force the water to wherever it might be needed.

Much of life aboard ship would depend on electricity produced by six steam-powered generators in the engine and boiler rooms. If these failed for any reason, two diesel-powered generators on the upper decks would automatically take over. While these were getting up to speed, the lights and public address system would be kept on by two small generators run by battery-powered electric motors.

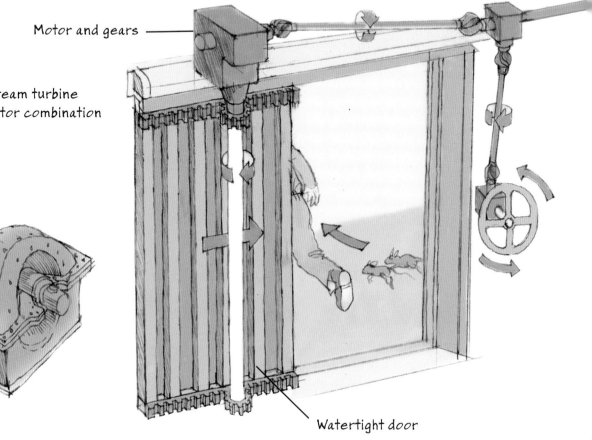

Motor and gears

Watertight door

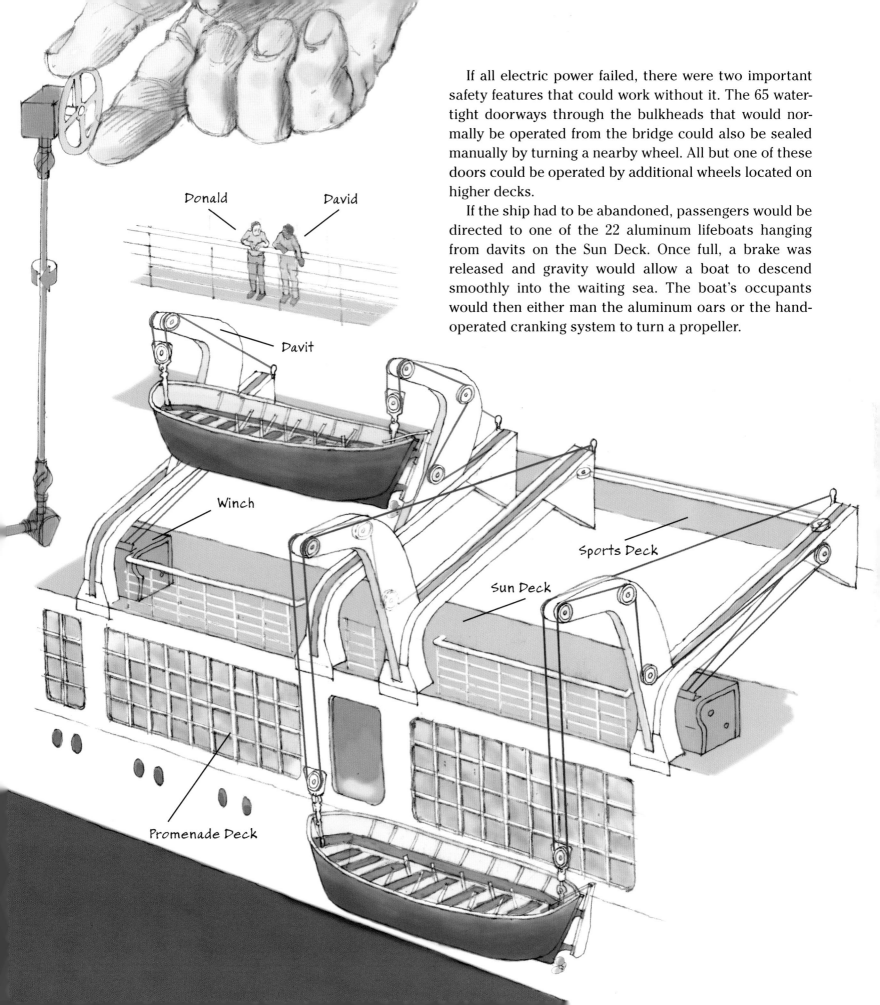

If all electric power failed, there were two important safety features that could work without it. The 65 water-tight doorways through the bulkheads that would normally be operated from the bridge could also be sealed manually by turning a nearby wheel. All but one of these doors could be operated by additional wheels located on higher decks.

If the ship had to be abandoned, passengers would be directed to one of the 22 aluminum lifeboats hanging from davits on the Sun Deck. Once full, a brake was released and gravity would allow a boat to descend smoothly into the waiting sea. The boat's occupants would then either man the aluminum oars or the hand-operated cranking system to turn a propeller.

Donald

David

Davit

Winch

Sports Deck

Sun Deck

Promenade Deck

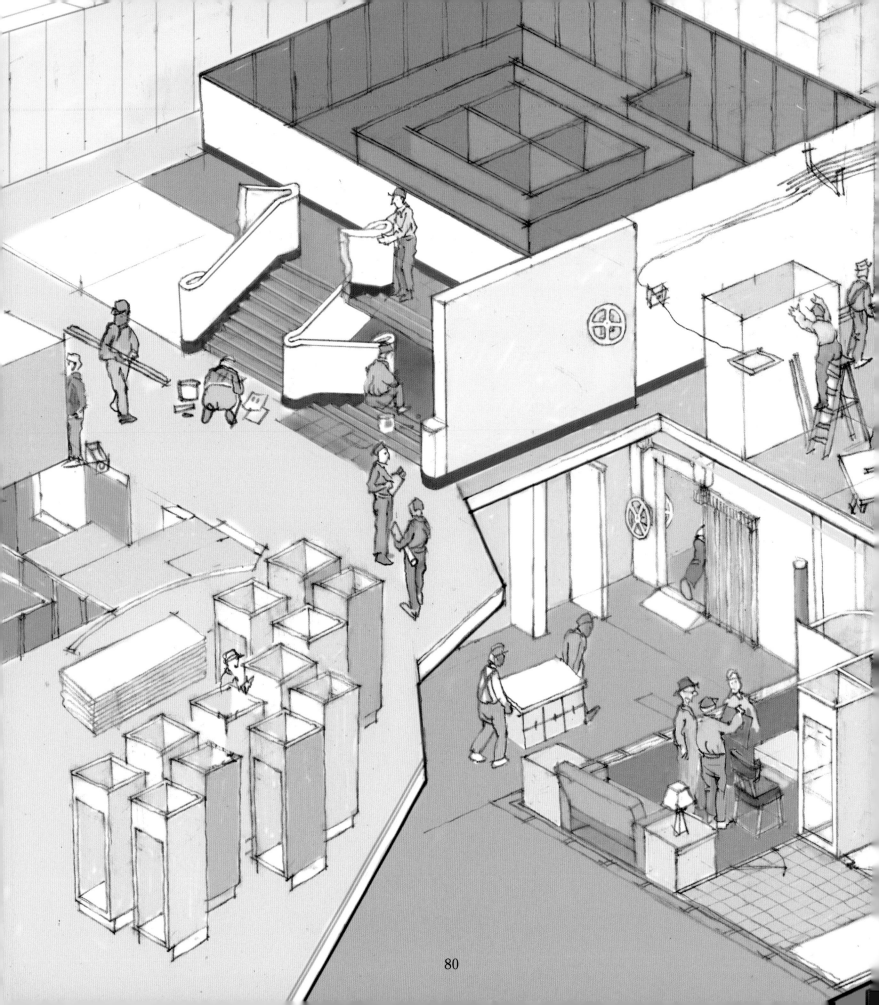

Over the next 12 months, 3,000 workers labored around the clock to complete the ship's interior. There were 40 public rooms, including two movie theaters and three dining rooms, one for each class. There were 340 crew spaces complete with bunks and lockers and almost 700 passenger staterooms. These were enclosed by a combination of modular panels and preassembled closets, all made of Marinite, as was much of their furniture.

Pipes were hooked up to bathroom fixtures, ducts to vents, and wiring to lights and thermostats. Interior floors were covered with asbestos tile or carpet. Curtains were hung and the public spaces were decorated. Everything was fireproof, including the paint on the walls.

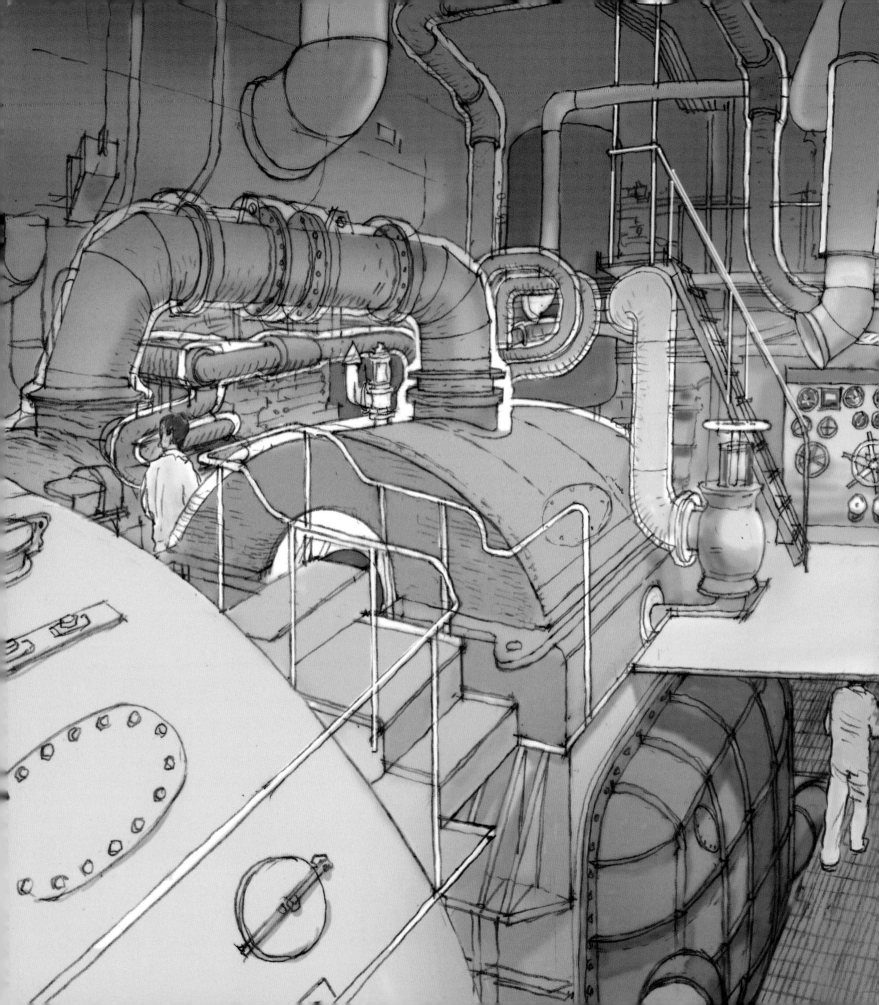

By mid-May it was time to test the ship's performance at sea. Since steam at almost 1,000 degrees would soon be flowing between the boilers and the turbines, many of the pipes between them were sheathed in asbestos material to contain the heat and protect the engineers stationed nearby. Wheels on the main control panels would be turned to open and close the steam pipes in response to orders from the bridge. Rows of gauges in all four boiler and engine rooms monitored the performance of all the equipment. A continuous record of the ship's performance was kept in a logbook on the desk in the center of both engine rooms.

The first trial, called the builder's trial, would test the ship's speed as well as the coordination between the bridge and the engine room. It was performed over a five-mile course about a hundred miles off the Virginia coast. Battling strong winds and rough seas, the ship effortlessly reached the speed it would need to beat *Queen Mary*. But as it approached 40 miles per hour, oil in two of the reduction gears showed signs of overheating. To avoid damage, the captain ordered the engineers to reduce steam to the turbines and return to port.

Three weeks later *United States* returned to sea for a second set of tests, called the owner's trial. While powering the ship at top speed, the turbines were suddenly reversed to see how long it would take for the ship to come to a stop—or fall apart. The stress on the propulsion system was enormous, but the equipment performed flawlessly. The test was then repeated in the opposite direction: traveling backward at full speed and then abruptly switching to full speed ahead.

Gibbs's masterpiece passed both tests with flying colors and returned to Newport News to complete the fitting out. The ship was due in New York on June 21 to meet the rest of its 900-person crew and get ready for voyage number one, eastbound.

Binnacle: houses the ship's compass

Radar screen: displays information from the radar mast

Both wheels can be used to turn the rudder.

The right wheel can work on autopilot.

Handle to operate
the windshield wiper

Smoking flares mark
the beginning and end of
the course for the trial

Telegraph: sends
instructions for engine
speed to the engine room

Funnel

Beauty parlor

Swimming pool

United States was equipped like a large hotel. There was a swimming pool to be shared by first- and cabin-class passengers (though not at the same time), and an attached gym. There was a kitchen for each class, and plenty of space for storing food. One of the refrigerated areas was dedicated to west-bound meat and another to eastbound meat—and another to kosher meat, which apparently didn't care which way it was going. Each class had its own lounges as well as smoking and reading rooms, beauty par-lors, and barbershops. Each cabin was equipped with its own telephone, and a switchboard on the main deck handled both onboard and long-distance calls. Playrooms were provided for children in each class, along with a kennel for dogs and cats of all classes.

First-class playroom

Crew kitchen

Unpacking SS *United States*

Imagine a knife cutting right down the center of the ship from stern to bow. Everything the knife passes through is visible on this profile drawing, but things along the sides of the ship do not appear. I've drawn some of the more important ones in front of the profile, for example the lifeboats (2 of the 24). I've also added part of the long glassed-in promenade and the hull below it, along with the hospital, radio room, and one of the luxurious first-class suites. During a voyage, almost every part of the ship is occupied, and since something is always happening somewhere, I've also combined daytime and nighttime activities.

All the spaces are numbered and grouped by deck. Each also has a frame number. To find something on the list, just slide your finger along the deck until you are above the small white frame number below the hull.

FUNNEL

1 Lookout window (for spotting submarines and other threats) 150

2 Steam horns (2 in forward stack, 1 in aft stack) 130

3 Soot extractors to clean exhaust 136

4 Engineers' overalls drying after being washed 146

5 Radio antenna (between funnels) 155

RADAR MAST

6 Rotating radar reflectors 107

7 Crow's nest/lookout 107

8 The only way up 109

9 Hatch to radar mast used in bad weather 106

NAVIGATION BRIDGE DECK

10 Elevator machinery 148

11 Emergency diesel-powered generator 142

12 Fan room for collecting fresh air 129

13 Tourist Class open deck 125

14 Tourist Class covered deck 122

15 Spiral crew stairs from Navigation Bridge Deck to B Deck 111

16 Chart room 102

17 Wheelhouse 97

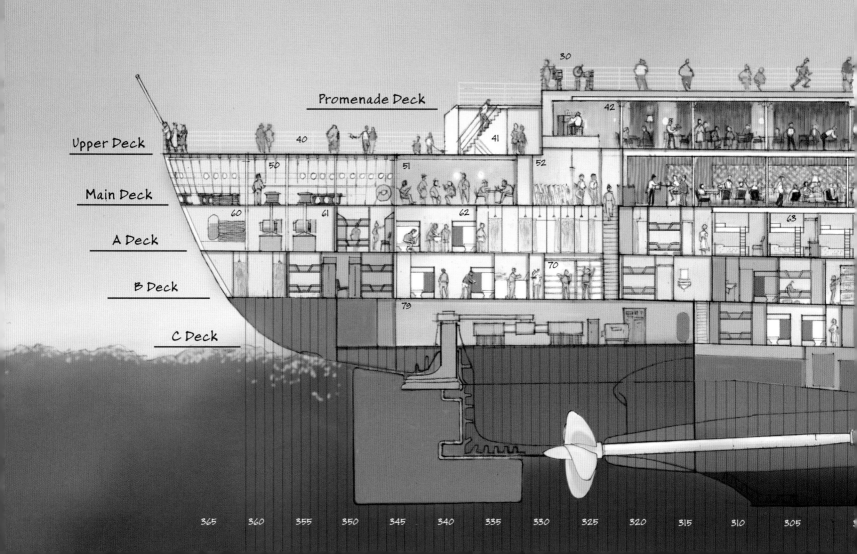

SPORTS DECK

SUN DECK

PROMENADE DECK

UPPER DECK

On July 3, 1952, shortly after noon, tugboats guided *United States* away from New York's Pier 86 and out into the Hudson River. Among its 1,660 passengers were Mr. and Mrs. William Francis Gibbs (Frederic had chosen to sit this one out and run the business). By 2:20 that afternoon, the ship had passed the lightship *Ambrose*, marking the official starting line for a possible record-setting crossing. Three days, 10 hours, and 40 minutes later, it passed Bishop Rock, the finish line at the entrance to the English Channel. Its average speed was 41 miles per hour. *Queen Mary*'s highest average speed had been about 36½ mph. Strips of black paint torn off *United States*'s hull near the waterline suggested a clear lack of favoritism on the part of the North Atlantic Ocean.

Four days later, *United States* set off on the more challenging westbound route and broke the record in that direction, too, with an average speed of 39.7 mph. With this crossing, the ship earned the Blue Riband, the accolade William Francis had been dreaming of for almost 35 years—and one it would never have to relinquish.

Over the next five years, the ship made 117 round trips between New York City and Europe and carried over 380,000 passengers from every walk of life. Among them were immigrants, artists, writers, performers, students, tourists, businessmen, princes and princesses, one emperor, one ocelot, the *Mona Lisa*, movie stars, countless much-loved pets, and a handful of politicians. The ship carried military officers and their families to and from postings overseas, but that was the closest it ever came to being called up for troop duty.

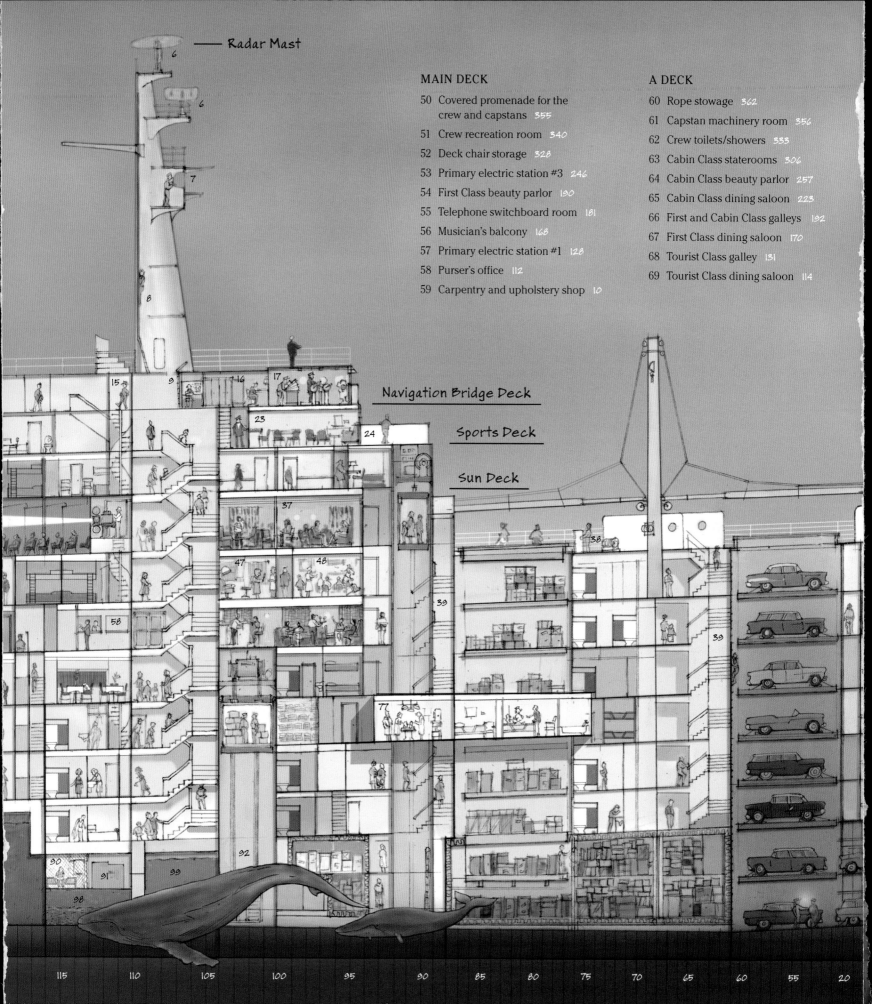

— Radar Mast

Navigation Bridge Deck

Sports Deck

Sun Deck

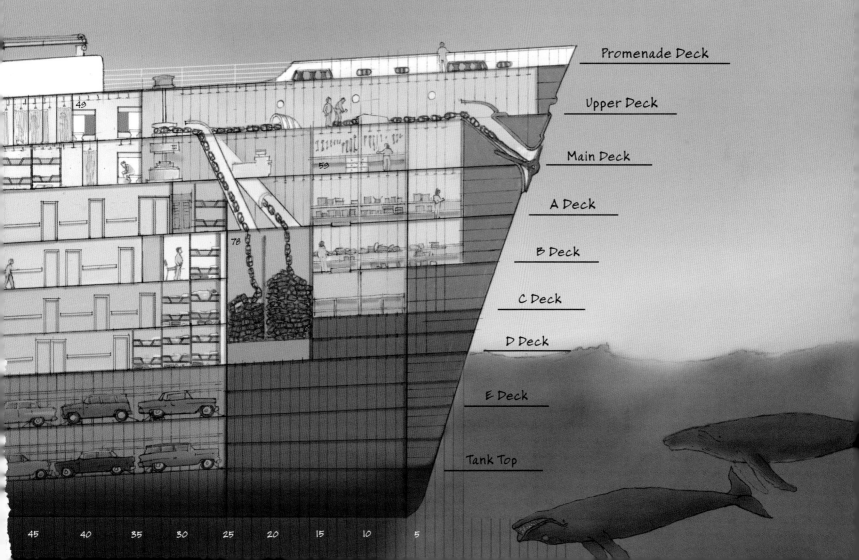

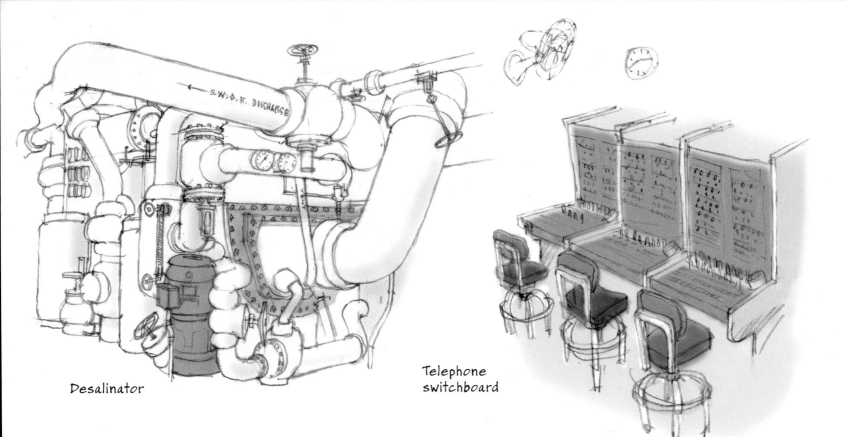

Desalinator

Telephone
switchboard

Because this hotel was out of reach of land, it also had to be completely self-sufficient. There was a print-shop in which a daily paper was created from news telegraphed to the ship during the voyage. On B Deck there was a hospital complete with a fully equipped operating room. On E Deck, in the refrigerated cargo hold there was a two-drawer, stainless-steel morgue with seven wooden caskets. And in case anyone got too out of control, a brig with two small cells was tucked behind one of the fuel-oil tanks. The operating room, morgue, caskets, and brig were available to all classes on a first-come-first-served basis.

Morgue

Operating room

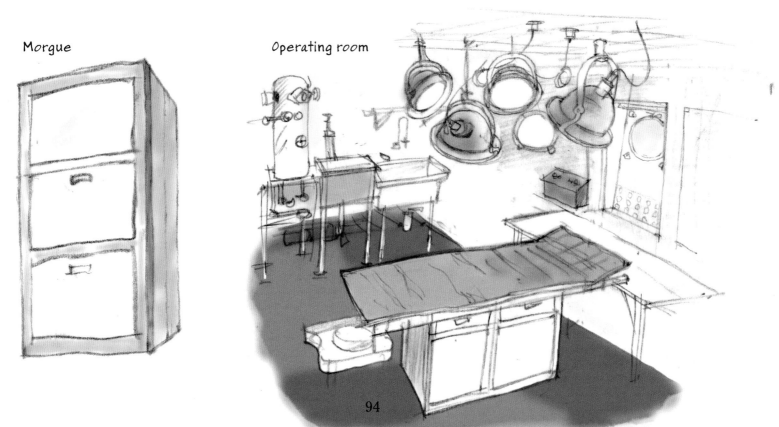

Funnel

Voyage 118 eastbound left New York on September 18, 1957. Two days later, the bridge received a distress call from a nearby Coast Guard cutter. A young machinist was in urgent need of medical attention. Commodore Anderson, the ship's captain, promptly changed course to meet up with the cutter. After a short lifeboat ride, the ailing seaman was hoisted through a cargo door on B Deck and delivered to the operating room. In no time, *United States* was back on course, only now carrying a passenger for Voyage 118's return *westbound*—minus his appendix.

4

THE FOLLOWING WEDNESDAY, the boat train from London's Waterloo Station pulled into one of the huge terminals at Southampton to drop off passengers who would join the recovering machinist on his homeward journey. Among them were the Macaulays of Bolton.

My mother, sister, brother, and I gathered our belongings and, after getting the family passport and visa inspected one more time, joined the line of tourist-class passengers slowly making their way toward a large, open doorway.

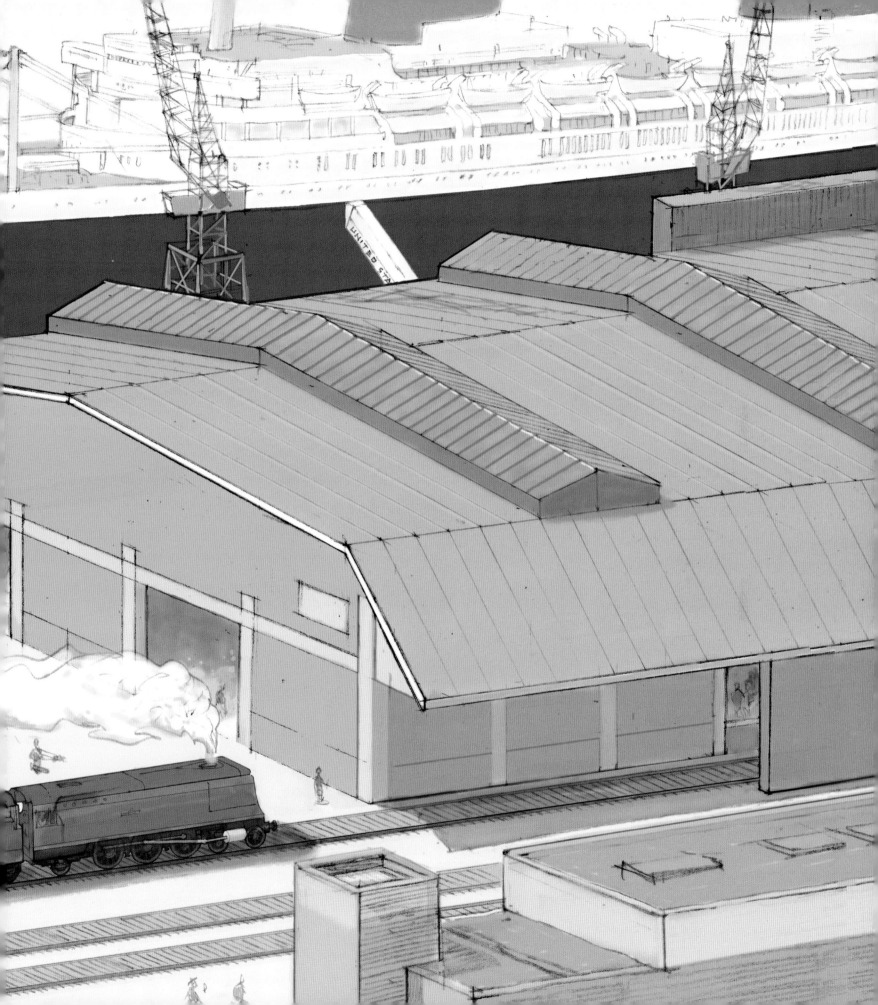

Standing in front of us and stretching out of sight in both directions was the towering black-and-white wall of the ship. It was the biggest thing I'd ever seen. A carpet ended at the bottom of a steep ramp, where a ship's photographer took one of only two pictures that could prove we were ever on the ship.

At the top of the ramp, a bellboy led us to a staircase. The words MAIN DECK were embedded in the floor. We followed him down to the letters B DECK and then along a corridor lined with doors. On the way he pointed out the toilets, which we were familiar with, and something else called a shower—which we were not.

Finally, we reached our cabin, B-105. On the tickets and labels it was called a stateroom, which had made it sound a lot bigger. But with its bunk beds and porthole, the room seemed perfect to me.

Before disappearing, the bellboy opened a miniature deck plan and drew a line from B-105 to the closest stairwell and elevator to help us find the restaurant—the next item on our agenda.

Lunch was served at 12:15. "Families with children are encouraged to be prompt." No prompting was necessary in our case, as we'd been up for hours. Deck plan in hand, we set off in search of table number 24 in what was officially called the Tourist Class Dining Saloon. "Sausage" was the most familiar item on the menu, so we all picked it. That's when I first met bologna and salami.

After lunch, we climbed the stairs to the words PROMENADE DECK to look around and get some fresh air. As the ship gently rocked, the four of us held on to the railing and watched England get smaller.

When my mother and brother went back inside, my sister and I decided to explore the rest of Tourist Class. We'd already seen most of it, with one significant exception: the tourist-class movie theater. We were just in time for Walt Disney's *Perri*, and it was free.

Later that afternoon, the ship docked in Le Havre to pick up more passengers. This was our first trip to France, so after dinner the four of us returned to the Promenade Deck for a peek. It looked just like England, but with different flags.

By the time we finally got back to our little stateroom, we were only too happy to climb into our bunks. It was two o'clock in the morning when the ship pulled away from the dock and began steaming toward the North Atlantic. None of us witnessed the departure.

The first thing I did the next morning—and every morning thereafter—was look through our porthole for a glimpse of the Empire State Building. It was all I could think about. Following breakfast that first day, my sister made a friend, so I decided to take in the 10:30 showing of *Perri* and returned that afternoon to see *Pajama Game*.

The shortage of opportunities for catastrophe on the ship suited my mother perfectly. She realized that my sister and I would be completely safe in the limited realm of Tourist Class. This allowed her to spend the next few days under a blanket on an aluminum deck chair, feeling increasingly seasick while clinging to our four-year-old brother so he didn't blow overboard.

Back on the Promenade Deck, I stared pathetically at the windows of the bridge, hoping for an invitation to go up and try the wheel. On dry land, this trick had gotten me into a signal box near a railway station in Wales. My performance at sea was apparently less convincing.

Perhaps the captain was too busy watching the traffic.

Friday and most of Saturday passed without incident or excitement. *Perri* and *Pajama Game* were still playing and my building remained out of sight.

The only difference between the days was that each felt longer than the one before. As it turns out, this was more than just a feeling. Every night while we slept, the ship's clocks were turned back at least an hour. This was done to prepare passengers for New York time, but it was also a form of torture if you were a seasick mother trapped on a rolling vessel for five days with three children to look after.

Saturday night was Gala Night. When confronted by the special menu, my mother put on a brave face. "Pâté de Foie Gras," "Mushrooms à la Française," "Queen Olives" (I wondered how many funnels), and "Gaspé Salmon au Four," were all available. I settled for French Ice Cream and Chocolate Sauce and wore a cone on my head. This was when the second photograph was taken.

On Monday morning, our porthole offered a completely different view. The horizon was now much closer, and there were things on it. Around six o'clock, I was permitted to go up on deck. I could make out the shapes of buildings and even some trees, but still, incredibly, there was no sign of the tallest building in the world!

That same morning, before going to the office, William Francis Gibbs was driven to the Brooklyn shoreline to welcome home the love of his life. It was a ritual he rarely missed. As far as I know, this was the only time he and I stood face-to-face.

The first buildings of Manhattan to come into view were those overlooking the Battery. I saw at least two that resembled "mine," but neither was quite right. It wasn't until we turned up the Hudson River that I finally saw it. I wasn't disappointed.

I was devastated.

It was nowhere near as big as I'd been promised by that illustration in my *Encyclopedia of Science for Boys and Girls*—the book I treasured, the book I trusted, the book I had personally selected for precious trunk space.

I was still in shock when we pulled alongside Pier 86 and I finally saw my waiting father. At least he was the same size as in England! Once reunited, we followed our luggage to a pair of huge station wagons to begin the last leg of the journey. My eyes were fixed on our surroundings, as I kept hoping for another look at the building. Perhaps somehow I still hadn't seen the real thing. But in no time we entered a tunnel that ran under the river we'd just sailed up.

Waiting on the other side was New Jersey, with a brilliant blue sky, wide highways, and lots of traffic. I had never seen so many cars, and they were all huge. They were also driving on the wrong side of the road. Fortunately, so were we.

Eventually our convoy left the highway and continued down narrower streets. The houses were not all made of brick or stuck together in long rows, like they were in Bolton. They came in different sizes, shapes, and colors. And there were trees on every street and in every yard.

Five days later, while I was busy exploring my new neighborhood, just nine miles away a spotless *United States* was steaming toward the Atlantic. Voyage 119 was already under way.

Gradually life settled into a pattern of new routines and occasional surprises. My walk to school took me over a railroad crossing, and on one particularly clear day, I saw in the distance the unmistakable silhouette of the Empire State Building. Then one night as I walked home from Boy Scouts across those same tracks, I noticed a flashing light and realized it must be coming from the top of the building.

Any lingering disappointment about our first encounter instantly vanished and in its place came a reassuring feeling I can still remember over 60 years later. The tallest building in the world, having lured me across the Atlantic Ocean under false pretenses, was keeping an eye on me day and night as this foreign land became home.

AFTERWORD

NO SURPRISE, it was the airplane that finally sank the superliners, along with the rising costs of labor, fuel, tickets, and time. People like my father had to get to work. Five days at sea was no longer a necessity, it was a luxury—or, if you asked my mother, an experience to be avoided at all costs.

But in Philadelphia, just five miles from where young William Gibbs saw his first ship launch, the product of his vision still bobs up and down in the Delaware River. SS *United States* hasn't sailed under its own power since 1969. While *Queen Mary*, the ship it defeated, basks in southern California sun thanks to some imagination and a lot of hard work, the "world champion" hides behind stacks of containers and is most easily seen from the Ikea cafeteria while scarfing down Swedish meatballs. The fact that it can be seen at all is testament to the willpower, stubbornness, and optimism of those who believe that it has survived this long for a reason. But as elegant and impressive as SS *United States* still is, it is locked in a race with time. Curling sheets of once-glistening black paint are slowly but certainly abandoning ship. If the skin is bailing, can the flesh and bones be far behind?

As a society with its eyes set on the future, we must look back from time to time to see where we've been and to be reminded of our accomplishments. This is why we have to leave some landmarks, both physical and emotional, in our wake—important things that people just like us fashioned from their dreams and built with their ingenuity and sweat. When these things outlive their original job descriptions, it's up to us to write new ones. SS *United States* is just such a landmark. It still has lessons to teach and inspiration to offer. But if it goes, those lessons become stories disconnected from reality, and that inspiration becomes wishful thinking destined to be lost with memory.

When I visit my publishers in New York, I travel by train, a once-glorious form of transportation that has itself been scuttled to within an inch of its life by the highway builders, car manufacturers, and shortsighted policy makers of past generations. As I approach the city, I still stare through the windows for that first glimpse of "my" building, and then I watch it grow until I sink into the tunnels that lead to the dreariness and chaos of Penn Station. I flee this subterranean labyrinth as quickly as humanly possible and head for the Flatiron Building (also a landmark). But on my way, I stop and look up Fifth Avenue at the Empire State Building. Every time we see each other, I am transported.

WONDERS OF TODAY

Even in ancient times people were wonderful builders. Seven of the things they built were so remarkable that they are called the Seven Wonders of the World. Some of the Seven Wonders were tombs or temples, and some were giant statues. The walls of a city were one of the wonders, and a lighthouse was another.

These ancient wonders were remarkable because in those days builders did not have giant machines to help them. They did not have steel and many of the other materials we have now to work with.

With our machines and our materials we have built many wonders. The pictures show some of them. How amazed the people of ancient times would be if they could see these wonders of ours!

Both the Empire State Building and SS UNITED STATES are shown in the illustration from my ENCYCLOPEDIA. I was oblivious to the technological triumph on which we were sailing; my eyes were set only on the Empire State Building and its imminent appearance, and it was years before I realized that that was our ship.

TIMELINE

1497 | The first well-documented crossing of the Atlantic from Europe to North America, by John Cabot in the sailing ship *Matthew,* takes 35 days.

Around 1710 | Thomas Newcomen (1664–1729) builds the first practical steam engine for pumping water out of mines.

1765 | James Watt (1736–1819) introduces his first improved steam engine designs, later manufactured and sold in partnership with Matthew Boulton.

August 22, 1787 | John Fitch (1743–1798) demonstrates the first successful steam-powered boat, *Perseverance,* on the Delaware River in Philadelphia.

February 21, 1804 | A locomotive designed by Richard Trevithick (1771–1833) makes the first recorded steam-powered railway journey.

May 1819 | First Atlantic crossing by a steam-powered ship, SS *Savannah.* Although equipped with steam engines, the ship made the voyage mostly under sail.

April 8–23, 1838 | The first steamship built specifically to carry passengers across the Atlantic, *Great Western,* makes its maiden voyage from Bristol, England, to New York in a time of 15 days, 12 hours.

August 24, 1886 | William Francis Gibbs is born in Philadelphia to parents William Warren Gibbs, a financier, and Frances Ayres Gibbs.

The Gibbs brothers, William Francis and Frederic (Susan Gibbs/SS *United States* Conservancy)

1919 | William Gibbs becomes chief of construction at the International Mercantile Marine Company. He surveyed the German-built liner *Vaterland,* which was later renamed SS *Leviathan* and used during World War I as a US troopship, then later refitted back into a passenger liner by Gibbs Brothers.

1922 | William Gibbs and his only brother, Frederic, start their naval architecture firm, Gibbs Brothers (renamed Gibbs & Cox in 1929, when they are joined by a third partner, Daniel Cox). The firm remains in business to this day, designing and engineering naval and other ships.

June 26, 1926 | SS *Malolo,* the first ocean liner designed by William Gibbs, is launched in Philadelphia.

August 31, 1939 | SS *America,* designed by William Gibbs for the passenger shipping company United States Lines, is launched in Newport News, Virginia. The ship made its maiden voyage in August 1940.

December 1941 | The United States declares war on Japan and its allies, joining World War II (which ended in 1945). *America* and other Gibbs-designed liners are converted to troop-carrying ships for the duration of the war.

April 1949 | United States Lines and the US government commission the designing of *United States* by Gibbs & Cox.

The first section of UNITED STATES's keel is lowered into place, February 8, 1950. (Richard Rabbett/SS *United States* Conservancy)

An aerial view of UNITED STATES nearing completion in dry dock, 1951. (Richard Rabbett/SS *United States* Conservancy)

Sea trials, May 1952 (SS *United States* Conservancy)

UNITED STATES departs New York on its maiden voyage, July 3, 1952, in a photograph taken from the window of Gibbs & Cox's offices.
(Robert G. Lenzer/SS *United States* Conservancy)

February 8, 1950 | Construction of SS *United States* begins with the laying of the first piece of the ship's keel.

June 23, 1951 | *United States* launches in Newport News, Virginia.

July 3–6, 1952 | *United States* makes its maiden voyage from New York to Europe, completing the transatlantic crossing in a record time of 3 days, 10 hours, and 40 minutes.

September 25–28, 1957 | The Macaulay family, including 10-year-old David, makes its first transatlantic journey, from Southampton to New York, aboard *United States*.

October 1958 | Scheduled passenger jet service across the Atlantic begins.

September 6, 1967 | William Gibbs dies in New York City at age 81.

October 1969 | *United States* makes its last transatlantic crossing, voyage number 400. In November the ship returned to Newport News for an overhaul, but was instead withdrawn from service and never sailed under its own power again.

Gala Night

1996 | *United States* is towed to Pier 84 in Philadelphia, where it remains. The ship was placed on the National Register of Historic Places in 1999.

2011 | *United States* is purchased by the SS *United States* Conservancy, which is dedicated to preserving the ship by renovating it as a permanent attraction and monument to the age of passenger ocean liners. The conservancy is an excellent source of information about the ship, its history, and its passengers and crew, as well as updates about plans for its future. ssusc.org

William Gibbs watches UNITED STATES arrive in New York Harbor.
(Marvin Koner/Getty Images)

ACKNOWLEDGMENTS

Special thanks to the following:

Susan Gibbs, for her unflagging willingness to answer or accurately redirect any question I fired her way, along with her sense of humor and support for this book throughout.

Steve Perry, for his formidable knowledge of SS *United States* (I mean that literally—be careful what you ask). As both teacher and student, he savored every opportunity to go back into his archives or the belly of the ship to find more answers to my endless list of questions.

For their willingness to share construction photographs and interior views of SS *United States*, William DiBenedetto and Mark Perry. For blueprints and artifacts belonging to William Francis Gibbs himself, my thanks to Tom Moore and the staff of the Mariners' Museum Library at Christopher Newport University and to the nearby Mariners' Museum itself, both in Newport News, Virginia.

For contemporary images of the ship, Kyle Ober, Brian Kitner, and Jeff Katz.

For both large blueprints and small details, Keith Harper at Gibbs & Cox in Newport News.

For firsthand information from the building site at Newport News Shipbuilding and Dry Dock Company during the construction of the ship, Alyn Fife, a shipwright who worked on SS *United States*.

For firsthand information about the ship's operation, Joseph Rota, who satisfied the duties of bellboy, ship's photographer, and usher in the Tourist Class movie theater; and ship's engineers Robert Sturm and Nicholas Landiak, who helped keep the ship running.

Jim Rindfleisch, caretaker of the ship as it languished at Newport News before moving to Philadelphia, who happily and generously responded to each request for more information, including a list of typical food supplies for a single voyage.

Online: Norwegian Heritage, although focused primarily on emigrant ships from Norway to America, often supplied additional details and images; Dan Trachtenberg for guided tours of the ship in a pair of videos created to record the countless details of its interior before and after stripping (and I mean countless); a growing number of "home movies" made by travelers on various transatlantic crossings and presented by Mark Perry and his Ship Geek productions; the Boston Public Library, which has a beautiful collection of photographs of SS *Leviathan*; and Wikipedia, an excellent source of ship biographies and appropriate cross-connections and references.

Simon Boughton, my publisher and editor who patiently watched various deadlines come and go, but who throughout the process asked consistently insightful questions and provided much-needed encouragement.

From the book world, or at least my part of it: Melanie Kroupa, Linda Davis, and Susan Bloom, all of whom reacted to earlier versions of the manuscript with thoughtfulness and enthusiasm, even as I began to lose my way.

To my dear and generally stoic wife, Ruthie Murray, who welcomed the project in its earliest stages, grew understandably frustrated when, after four years, I continued expressing my uncertainty about the venture, only to emerge with me from the darkness with her critical eye and objectivity restored in time to improve the finished drawings.

And finally, to Joan and James Macaulay, my parents, who have supported all my efforts over the years, but who were particularly eager to see this one come to fruition. Although my father did not actually sail on the ship, their decision to emigrate to the United States in 1957 gave my sister and brother and I access to opportunities that simply weren't on the horizon, or at least as plentiful, in postwar England. To them, this story is dedicated.

SELECTED READING

Agricola, Georgius, *De Re Metallica*. Translated by Herbert Clark Hoover and Lou Henry Hoover. New York: Dover Publications, 1950.

Baker, Elijah, III, *Introduction to Steel Shipbuilding*. New York: McGraw Hill, 1953.

Braynard, Frank O., *The Big Ship: The Story of the S.S. United States*. New York: Turner Publishing, 2011.

Ellis, C. Hamilton, *The Lore of Ships*. New York: Crescent Books, 1978.

———, *The Lore of the Train*. New York: Crescent Books, 1971.

Friedel, Robert, *A Culture of Improvement: Technology and the Western Millennium*. Cambridge, MA: MIT Press, 2007.

Maxtone-Graham, John, *SS United States: Red, White, & Blue Riband, Forever*. New York: W. W. Norton, 2014.

Sturm, Robert C., *SS United States: The View from Down Below*. Medford, NY: Robert C. Sturm, 2015.

Swanson, William Elmer, *Modern Shipfitter's Handbook*. 2nd ed. New York: Cornell Maritime Press, 1941.

Ujifusa, Steven, *A Man and His Ship: America's Greatest Naval Architect and His Quest to Build the S.S. United States*. New York: Simon & Schuster, 2012.

Aboard UNITED STATES in Philadelphia, June 2014: The author looks out from a hatch in one of the ship's funnels.

(Kyle Ober/SS *United States* Conservancy)

Me

The Macaulay family boarding UNITED STATES, September 25, 1957.

For my parents, Joan and James Macaulay

Copyright © 2019 by David Macaulay
Published by Roaring Brook Press
Roaring Brook Press is a division of Holtzbrinck
Publishing Holdings Limited Partnership
175 Fifth Avenue, New York, NY 10010
mackids.com
All rights reserved

Page 124: Illustrations Harry McNaught; and Excerpt(s) from THE GOLDEN BOOK OF SCIENCE FOR BOYS AND GIRLS by Bertha Morris Parker, copyright © 1956, 1963 by Penguin Random House LLC. Used by permission of Golden Books, an imprint of Random House Children's Books, a division of Penguin Random House LLC. All rights reserved. Published in the United Kingdom as *The Encyclopedia of Science for Boys and Girls.*

Library of Congress Control Number: 2018039860
ISBN: 978-1-59643-477-6

The SS *United States* Conservancy leads the global effort to prevent "America's Flagship" from being lost forever. The Conservancy, a national nonprofit organization, supports the maintenance, restoration, and ultimate reuse of SS *United States.* It is also building the world's largest collection of art, artifacts, and documents from the ship so the world's fastest ocean liner will endure for generations to come. For more information, visit ssusc.org or wearetheunitedstates.org.

Our books may be purchased in bulk for promotional, educational, or business use. Please contact your local bookseller or the Macmillan Corporate and Premium Sales Department at (800) 221-7945 ext. 5442 or by email at MacmillanSpecialMarkets@macmillan.com.

First edition, 2019
Book design by Angela Corbo Gier
Printed in China by RR Donnelley Asia Printing Solutions Ltd.,
Dongguan City, Guangdong Province

1   3   5   7   9   10   8   6   4   2